To: Joe

We're looking forward t
jellybean!

Love,
The Buders

Christmas 1995

DOUG WEBSTER

Dear
Dad

DOUG WEBSTER

Dear Dad

A
JANET
THOMA
BOOK

THOMAS NELSON PUBLISHERS
Nashville • Atlanta • London • Vancouver

Published in Nashville, Tennessee, by Thomas Nelson, Inc., Publishers, and distributed in Canada by Word Communications, Ltd., Richmond, British Columbia.

The Bible version used in this publication is THE NEW KING JAMES VERSION. Copyright © 1979, 1980, 1982, 1990, Thomas Nelson, Inc., Publishers.

The research for this book was conducted among 1,500 children and adults across the United States. To protect the privacy of individuals who are quoted or referenced in this book, all names and certain identifying details have been changed. No reference to any person, living or dead, is intended and any use of the names of actual persons is purely coincidental. While true names and specific details have been changed, the meaning has been preserved.

Library of Congress Cataloging-in-Publication Data

Webster, Doug.
    Dear Dad: If I could tell you anything— : Doug Webster.
      p. cm.
    Includes bibliographical references.
    ISBN 0-7852-8079-0
    1. Fatherhood.   2. Fathers.   I. Title.
HQ756.W42   1995
360.874′2—dc20   94-44257
                                                CIP

Printed in the United States of America
1 2 3 4 5 6 — 00 99 98 97 96 95

To Brookelyn, Jamie, and Chase. Your presence in my life has granted me the most cherished position—Dad. May you forever hear these words from me: "You're mine, I love you, and I am so proud of you!"

Special thanks to an incredible lady, Robin Webster. Our children are the result and proof of my deep love for you, my wife and their mom.

A final epiphany to George C. Webster, i.e., Dad. May my words "by George" offer my sincere thanks and love to you.

CONTENTS

PART FOUR

PART FIVE

ACKNOWLEDGMENTS

Like having and raising children, book writing is never a solo flight. I would like to thank the following people for their valuable and gifted contributions to *Dear Dad*.

To Janet Thoma for your willingness to put your respected signature and your touch of excellence on this important work.

To Amy Glass and the unsung heroes at Thomas Nelson Publishers for doing such quality work and making me look better than ought to be legal.

To Jim Burns for your constant partnership in our shared life and work. Your presence as a friend, model dad, and colleague give my life great value.

To Tom Kowalski who, by his choice of love, became my loving stepdad, dad away from home, and friend.

To Bob Glick who, by my choice of love, became my respected father-in-law, third dad, and friend.

To Laurie Pilz who remained diligent, sane, and enthusiastic as we journeyed through a ton of comments from the kids. Your partnership in my life's work is a gift.

PART
ONE

If I could tell you anything . . .

WHAT KIDS SAY . . .

I like my dad. He's a neat guy.
Jenny, age unknown

I'm glad you're my father.
Kiersten, age sixteen

Dad, can we talk please? I asked you that one day as a freshman, and you said you were busy that day because you had to go to surgery. You never came back to talk to me. Four years later, I've given up waiting for you.
Ann, age eighteen

WHAT KIDS MEAN . . .

I love you.

I am grateful.

I need you to listen to me.

WHAT KIDS NEED . . .

A dad who loves.

A dad who listens.

A dad who knows he matters to his children.

CHAPTER 1

> *Dear Dad,*
>
> *You matter.*
>
> *Love,*
> *Your child*

YOU MATTER.

Dad, you are my hero. I hope I can be like you as a father, husband, and friend.
Joseph, age seventeen

I love you and thanks for being so understanding, funny, cool to my friends, and for sticking up for me. You're the best!
Brenda, age fourteen

Not long ago I was speaking at a youth camp. While I was working my way through a lunch of mysterious camp food a young teenage girl named Jenny walked by me, stopped, spun around, and blurted out, "You remind me of my dad."

"Oh . . . ," I said with curious concern. I then realized I have entered a new season of life. I no longer remind a thirteen-year-old of her big brother. Now, I make her think of her dad.

With the touch of a highly trained bomb-squad technician, I delicately probed for an explanation. "What makes you say that?"

"Well, you look like him. And he wears those same shorts and ankle socks, and he has short brown hair."

"So, is it good or bad that I remind you of your dad?" I ventured as if clipping a wire of dynamite.

"Yeah, it's good. I like my dad. He's a neat guy."

"It's true," her friend chimed in.

"Wow! I hope my daughters say that about me when they're teenagers," I told the girls.

The young teen spun around again and headed for the door. Throwing her hair off her shoulders with the flip of her head, she looked back at me and said, "Yeah, my dad's pretty cool . . . sometimes." She flashed a victorious smile and paraded out with her friend.

Boom! I guess I can't expect miracles.

I was touched by Jenny's comment. I love to hear kids speak about their dads, especially when it is positive. Being a dad myself and having spent years working with young people, I have discovered a penetrating truth: *You matter.*

What comes from dads finds a short, uninterrupted path to the hearts of our children . . . even older children.

I've learned this firsthand. I have three children, and I've discovered a great deal about my influence on these precious kids. The first two in our family circle were girls: Brookelyn and Jamie. (My dad, who grew up in Brooklyn, asked, "How can you name a kid after a city like that?" I tell him, "Easy, Dad. First, we spell it with an *E* after the *K*. Plus, I grew up in southern California. To me, Brooklyn is a bridge and a TV show.")

Our girls are sweet, fun-loving, delightful people who have melted my heart. One of the highlights of my day is coming home and hearing them scream, "Daddy! Daddy's home!" (Mom does a good job as my PR agent when I'm not home.)

The third child is a boy: Chase. Although I considered calling him Bronx, I avoided my father's further inquisition and simply named him after the most common activity I would do throughout the first few years of his life. Now that I have a boy, I realize Chase will look to me to learn how to be a decent male as well as a decent human being. My wife, Robin, and I have gone from man-to-man to zone defense now that we have three children. Inevitably, though, one kid will make a fast break and score on us, and we know there's no third parent waiting to come out of the penalty box in a few minutes to give us some relief.

In the process of fathering, I have learned a frightening fact: I matter to my kids. They treasure my relationship with them. I have tremendous influence over their lives. I am over-whelmed, humbled, and scared by this, and I doubt that I am the only dad who feels this way. Here's what I have discovered about being a dad that no one told me in Lamaze classes:

- I'm a novice at this dad stuff because I've never been a dad before.
- I'm hard-pressed to find a dad worth modeling.
- My dadhood is undermined by limited time. I'm busy striving to make a living and—I hope—some differ-ence in the world.
- I feel tremendous financial pressure. It's expensive to raise a family.
- There are times when I feel like an outsider with my kids.
- I want to love and influence my kids more than anything.

I wish all kids spoke about their dads as Jenny did. Yet that's not the case; other young people reply as Ann did. I met Ann at a school conference; a sharp, self-confident girl, she was the center of attention for a group of girls and a few interested guys. As I talked to the group, I asked them about their future plans. Ann spoke up quickly. "I want to be a cook," she said. She then looked at me as if baiting a challenge.

I responded, "Great."

"You think that's a waste, don't you?" Ann retorted.

"No," I said. "You sound as if you know what you want to do. Good for you."

"Well," Ann said, "I am going to work at a German restaurant so I can learn about the culture. I have been studying German, and I want to learn more before I go to med school."

I was even more impressed. "Why med school?"

"I plan to be a neurologist."

"Big plans! Why do you want to be a neurologist?" I asked her. By now she was the only one speaking. One boy had disappeared; he was probably too intimidated to pursue a girl who studied foreign cultures on her way to medical school.

"My dad's an endocrinologist," Ann replied.

Her future plans and my attentive listening prompted the other young people to share their post–high school plans.

Then I said, "Now I need your help. I have three kids at home. I really want to be a good dad for them. What advice do you have for me as a father?"

The young people seemed caught off guard. Adults seldom ask teens for guidance. They all shared various comments—all, that is, except Ann.

"What about you, Ann?"

"I don't really have any advice," she mumbled.

I was shocked by her silence since she had been so vocal before.

"Come on, Ann," I coaxed. "You've got to have a few thoughts for me." I was thinking about how she wanted to mimic her dad's profession. Her answer surprised me.

Ann told me of a time four years prior when she really needed to talk with her dad, but he was on his way to work. She promised it would take only a few minutes. Yet he denied her request and said, "We'll talk later." Later never came. She then looked at me and talked as if her dad stood in my shoes:

Dad, can we talk please? I asked you that one day as a freshman, and you said you were busy that day because you had to go to work. You never came back to talk to me. Four years later, I've given up waiting for you.

I wish her dad could have heard her that day. As a man trained to bring healing to people through medicine, I've got to believe he would give anything to mend this one young broken heart. I found myself hurting for him, and I also felt afraid for myself. Would my kids someday tell some adult about the hurts in their relationship with me? I prayed not.

Having worked with young people for more than fifteen years as a youth worker, speaker, and now as executive director of the National Institute of Youth Ministry, I have had the privilege of being an insider in the world of children and adolescents. They let me in without realizing I also represent a potential enemy: parents. I guess I ought to wear a blue helmet and call myself a member of the UN peacekeeping contingent. Peace treaties and open communication are most needed between parents and children, especially teenagers. And we dads are often the farthest removed from the peace talks. We need ambassadors who can build a bridge between child and dad. I offer you that bridge.

I'm not coming to you as an expert on fatherhood. I don't have a Ph.D. in "Daddiology." (Anybody who claims to be an expert on parenting doesn't have kids. We are never in control of our kids, nor do we ever master them.) But I have credibility; I'm a dad. I've learned a lot I want to pass on to you. Maybe as I share some of the insights I've gained you'll discover an idea or a practical tool to help you draw closer to your children. If they are like the thousands of kids I have been with, they don't need much incentive to draw close to you.

Over the years I have counseled numerous students like Ann. If I develop a rapport with them, I'll ask them about their relationship with their dads. Some young people speak out of respect and love. One question opens the heart more than any other question I ask: *If you could tell your dad anything, what would you say?* Some can't find anything to say. Other times there is no dad to speak of and instead kids describe a stepdad or someone else.

This book is not comprised of one man's opinion. The content of *Dear Dad* comes from more than fifteen hundred young people and adults who participated in my written surveys, face-to-face interviews, and counseling. Although the names and details have been changed to protect identities, the personal encounters described here have arisen from my years of working with young people. I've spent a lot of time helping kids reconnect with their God and with the people in their lives. That's why I ask them about their dads. I want to help them hear the feelings within their own hearts. They can also practice their answers with me in case their dads one day ask them the same question. When asked by a sincere, attentive, accepting person, kids speak up. I think you will benefit from what I've heard them say. I have.

I took a proactive approach with hundreds of young people and adults through a written survey. The survey was simple in structure so young people would be encouraged to participate. On the survey I asked three open-ended questions:

1. If I were to describe my dad with a color, he would be _____ because . . .

2. If I were to rate my relationship with my dad on a scale of one to ten (ten being the highest), mine would be a _____ because . . .

3. If I could say anything to my dad, I would tell him . . .

Although I was pleased to see the candid nature of the kids' replies, very few responses really surprised me. A few were so strong in language and tone that I can't reprint them in this book without being offensive. Their words revealed various feelings, including hope, fear, guilt, pride, and curiosity. But when I sorted them all out, I ended up with eleven key messages from kids:

I love you.
Please accept me.
Please don't hurt me.
Please stop hurting you.
Be with me.
Listen to me.
Please forgive me.
Be real with me.
Trust me.
Leave me alone.
Thank you, Dad!

We'll take a closer look at these eleven messages of a child's heart as each is discussed in a chapter of this book. But remember that none of these messages stands alone. They are interwoven throughout a progressive cycle of growth for children and their fathers. Like scenes from a great drama, a child moves from one act, or stage, to the next. I call the first stage the "monologue."

THE MONOLOGUE

Here, a child's cry of the heart is to be close enough to connect, not merely coexist with Dad. Five of the eleven messages describe that need to connect: *I love you, Accept me, Don't hurt me, Stop hurting you,* and *Be with me.* Each of these five messages is either saying *Draw me close* or *Don't push me away. I want to be near enough to you to connect with you.* A child needs to not just hear but also experience from Dad the message, *You're mine, and I want you close to me.*

Dads can best establish this connection with their children between birth and the preteen years. The monologue messages of the child's first cry of the heart, *Connect with me,* can be heard and answered long before the child reaches an age of reason. A heart-to-heart understanding can be developed before a mind-to-mind relationship. Five-year-old kids know when they are loved, accepted, and safe. They may not articulate their need to be with Dad, but they truly value and depend upon their time spent with him. (That's why many of the statements from the kids come from preteens and teens; the younger children feel these cries but can't verbalize them.)

Then again, young children, especially preschoolers, do have a way of communicating their desires: crying. Do they want a verbal response from us dads? No, just action. *Show me love and acceptance. Stop the hurting behavior. Spend time with me.* A dad's words are very valuable at this stage, but they are secondary. Attitude, tone, and action speak louder than words.

The monologue stage begins at birth and extends through a child's preteen years. In the monologue stage, kids are saying, *Here's what you need to hear from me.* In the next stage, the "dialogue" stage, kids are asking Dad to respond to them.

THE DIALOGUE

Relationships cannot be one-way. They demand give-and-take from both parties. As children enter their teenage years, they want more than to be near Dad. They want to relate with him. The father-child relationship is the segue for the child's entrance into the world of people and other relationships he or she will develop. Three of the eleven messages support the second cry of the heart, the desire to relate: *Listen to me, Please forgive me,* and *Be real with me.*

Each of these messages demands a dad in active pursuit of a relationship with his child.

The third stage of the drama, the "epilogue," occurs from the midteen years to the late-teen years, when the child's desire is to grow up and out from the family.

THE EPILOGUE

Like an arrow from the bow of an archer, every child must be released from the parent to become an adult. This third stage of the growth cycle is the epilogue, the last scene before the child enters a world of independence. The teenager in the epilogue stage has a final cry of the heart for Dad, *Release.* Middle teenagers push headstrong into this last stage with their cry for release, the final cry of the heart.

Two messages form the epilogue: *Trust me* and *Leave me alone.* They may be the flip side of the same coin, because a dad who doesn't hear the first message, *Trust me,* will eventually get the second message, *Leave me alone.* Part of this cry of release is a child's desire for a father's blessing. Children desperately desire a message from their fathers that says, *I am pleased with you.*

The kids' final message is expressed by one word: *Thanks.* I call this the "epiphany."

THE EPIPHANY

The epiphany is an annual celebration in the Christian church. The word describes a manifestation, or a revealing, of something believed. In our analogy of childhood growth, the epiphany stage celebrates the life given to a child by a father. It is, in short, a resounding cheer for what has been manifested. Child after child after child (even some with obvious pain from severed relationships with their fathers) told me he or she wanted to thank Dad. Picture an actor at the end of the drama of the growth cycle looking out to Dad, who sits cheering in the audience, and simply saying, *Thanks*.

Do you want a closer relationship with your child? I do. I not only want to love my children, I want the love to go both ways: I want to be loved by them too. And I need to hear them tell me that they love me, especially when life is tough. Those are the times when a "Dear Dad" letter or an "I love you, Daddy" hits home. Recently I came across a letter from a daughter to her father, who was struggling to survive his career's most embittered time. In his chosen career, his troubles were acted out on a stage for the whole world to watch. His daughter knew all that, so she left this note on his pillow, where he found it when he returned home from his office one night at 2 A.M.

Dear Daddy,

I love you. Whatever you do, I will support you. I am very proud of you. Please wait a week or even ten days before you make this decision. Go through the fire just a little bit longer. You are so strong! I love you.

Julie

Julie penetrated her dad's heart in a few words. She connected with her dad: *Dear Daddy*. She strengthened her relationship: *I love you*. Then she gave him release through a blessing: *I am very proud of you. You are so strong*. Her short letter touched him deeply. Her father said of the difficult decision facing him, "If anything could have changed my mind, Julie's note would have done it."[1]

On August 9, 1974, Richard Nixon resigned from the presidency of the United States. When he left office in disgrace, his heart was broken. His career was ruined. Still, the words of Julie's Dear Daddy letter rang clear. Her love was unimpeachable.

What would your child write in a Dear Dad letter to you?

My greatest purpose in writing this book is to give you an inside look at your child's heart so you will draw closer to your child, whatever his or her age. If I help you in any way as a dad, then my work over the years will have been fruitful. God bless you in what I consider to be one of life's most important and influential roles.

Dear Dad,

*You are the most impor-
tant man in my life. I love
you, and I need you.*

*Love,
Your child*

PART

TWO

THE
KIDS'
MONOLOGUE:

I want to connect with you.

WHAT KIDS SAY . . .

My dad loves me for the person I am, not who he wants me to be.
Catherine, age sixteen

My dad is like the color red—he's always angry.
Latitia, age fourteen

We do a lot together. I wish I could have known my dad when he was my age.
Alan, age seventeen

WHAT KIDS MEAN . . .

Accept me.

Don't hurt me.

I love you.

Be with me.

WHAT KIDS NEED . . .

A dad who accepts his child as he or she is.

A dad who doesn't hurt his child.

A dad who spends time with his child.

A dad who connects with his child and makes

him or her a more important part of his life.

CHAPTER 2

Dear Dad,

I love you.

Love,
Your child

I LOVE YOU.

I'm glad you're my dad.
Makenzie, age thirteen

I love you and forgive you.
Mark, age nineteen

I love you and wish I could express it more consistently.
Jody, age thirty-one

The hospital seemed cold and abandoned as I walked down the quiet corridor. A smell of rubbing alcohol added to my preexisting nausea. Fluorescent lights cast haunting shadows over the utilitarian furniture. Although this was not my first time in a hospital, the place felt foreign.

Arterial sclerosis. What on earth does that mean? I wondered. All I knew was that my dad was scheduled for quintuple bypass heart surgery the next day. As a young man just twenty years old, my understanding of death and illness was naive at best. I had been a child when both my grandfathers died years prior; my innocence then had kept me from truly knowing the wrenching pain of giving up someone I loved. Unfortunately this evening it seemed all too real. No more standing under the protection of a parent's comforting words and guiding strength. Now my dad faced life's ultimate challenge, and he would not be there to encourage and support me as I watched him endure it.

The conversation between us that night amounted to small talk:

"What time is the surgery?"

"First thing in the A.M."

"Really?"

"Yep."

"Do you have everything you need? . . . Can I get you anything?"

"No, I'm fine, son. I'll be all right."

Son. The word was probably the closest thing we had to an affectionate pet name. Every now and then he did call me "sport," a simple but significant nickname. Only one name meant trouble: Douglas Craig Webster. Then I knew I was in for a reckoning.

The words *son, dad,* and *daughter* say so much. They offer definition, legal standing, and love.

I stood in that dreary hospital, where my two brothers and, years later, my first two children had been born. Would it be the place of my dad's departure from this life?

I looked at my dad. He had always seemed big when I was growing up. Whatever their stature, dads stand tall in the minds of their children. Now, at five-foot-seven, my dad appeared small. Yet no matter how tall, how tough, how invincible a dad may be, death is a cruel sparring partner. For the first time in my life, I faced losing my dad. I felt alone.

The next words that came from my mouth were driven by something deep inside. My heart was crying out, and it took over before my brain could intercept my thoughts: *"Dad . . . I love you."*

My lips quivered. My palms became sweaty. My heart started racing. As though I were diving from a high platform into a small pool of water hundreds of feet below, I had taken the blind leap of faith that seldom had been attempted in my family. I had spoken three of life's most powerful, yet most difficult words: *I love you.*

I grew up in a family heavily influenced by our British background. My dad has traced our family tree beyond the United States to Barbados. On that small island my great grandfather found refuge from a difficult life in England. Stories of past Websters portray stoic men fighting their way from country to country in search of a better life. I dare not imply that every male from England is devoid of heart and emotion. It's just that in my limited experience, that was true.

My folks got a divorce when I was eight years old. My two brothers and I lived with Mom for a short time, then our parents decided it was best for us to be raised by Dad. That lasted for a while until my needs for nurturing were not met in our all-male household. At age nine, I took off for San Diego to live with my mother, just the two of us.

The new arrangement went as smoothly as possible for a single parent who was raising a young boy in an unknown town. Life grew more complicated when a new family— what became my stepfamily—entered our lives. Then, at age ten, my limited reasoning led me to believe life "at home" with Dad and my two brothers seventy-five miles to the north seemed less confusing. I packed up my few belongings, said good-bye to Mom, and returned to my dad's, an emotional prodigal looking for a home.

We four male Websters settled into what I now call "my early-bachelor days." I tell people, "We were four men living together, but we were all alone . . ."

Yet we never became the Brady Bunch. More aptly put, we were four males living in the same place, sometimes bumping into each other like porcupines in a barrel. I grew up fast. *I love you* was a seldom-exchanged phrase . . .

The hospital room was quiet. I stared at my dad. He looked up at me and immediately perceived my fear. With the healing, delicate touch of a highly skilled surgeon, my father responded, "Son, I love you too. I'll be OK. And I'll see you in the morning."

Thank God my dad was right.

Why is it so easy to say "I love you" to someone we've been dating for a few months, weeks, or even days, but so difficult to say those same words to family members with whom we've lived for decades? It's certainly that way for teenagers. Kids do love their parents, and parents do love their kids. We just don't hear about it very often.

I've got a message to relay to dads from their kids: *They love you.* Bottom line, far above any other message, kids have told me they love their dads. Some of them courageously love their dads, even though they've been through difficult times with them.

You've heard of childlike faith. I want to introduce you to childlike resilience. Kids keep loving and loving and loving. Of course, not all kids do, but many more than I might have guessed before I started asking and listening. Of 330 young people in one group that I surveyed, 49.7 percent used the word *love* when talking about their dads.

The first cry of the heart from our kids is *connect*. The best way kids know to communicate this message is through the primary message *I love you*. Here's how some of the kids put it:

If twelve-year-old Amber could say anything to her dad, she would tell him:

I love you, and I would give my life for you.

The color white best describes Amber's dad, she said, because

He is so pure and clean and loving.

On a scale of one to ten, Amber gives her dad a nine!

Amber's dad means more than anything in the world to her; he's worth her entire life.

If fifteen-year-old Bryan could say anything to his dad, he would say,

You're the best dad in the world, and even though you're a little weird, I love you.

He rates his relationship with his dad as an eight because, he said,

We get along well.

How does Bryan's dad do it? Bryan offers one expression of his dad's love:

He's always nice to me, and he's the only person who will gladly give me a ride if I ask for one.

To a fifteen-year-old, a chauffeur dad is a valuable resource, even if he's weird. Three cheers for us weird dads with driver's licenses! (If your department of motor vehicles photo is like mine, you even look weird on your license!)

When fourteen-year-old Darlene thinks of "Dad," her stepdad comes to mind. She gives him the color orange because, she said,

He stands out when he is around people, and he is a bright man.
After ranking him an eight on the scale, Darlene wrote,
He's my stepdad, and he cares about me and others.
Any thoughts for your stepdad, Darlene?
I love you.
What a glorious review for any dad to hear, especially a stepdad!

Twelve-year-old Daria rates her dad a ten because,
My dad and I love each other very much. I enjoy him as my dad.
He is best painted red, Daria said, because
Red is happy, and that's my dad.
Any comments to your dad, Daria?
You're the best dad ever!
I hope Daria's dad reads this book.

I could go on and on. I've found hundreds of kids who want to say "I love you" to their dads.

Children are tremendously resistant to the voices that say,
Don't trust him. Don't give him what's valuable to you.

Just last night I was speaking to a group of students about priorities and the use of money. I asked for a few volunteers to come up front and give me a dollar in exchange for something. The teenagers were leery. I had to persuade them of the value of what they would get for their dollar.

A funny thing happened. In the back of the room, four-year-old Craig was waving a one-dollar bill. I called him up front. As he approached me, some teenagers started yelling, "Don't give him the buck, Craig."

What did Craig do? He reached out his hand and gave me the dollar. No questions asked. When some kids a decade older would not even give me one lousy buck without knowing what they would first get from me, a four-year-old with childlike faith was ready to invest. You see, kids give us adults the benefit of the doubt. Craig was willing to trust me.

Our kids are like that four-year-old; they continue to reach out to us. Listen to what Luke, Carrie, Mary, and Andrea have to say:

Thirteen-year-old Luke pictured his dad as red because, Luke said,

He has a temper.

He ranks his relationship with his dad a two because he said his dad,

Calls me stupid, and says that I'm very idiotic.

Now I was thinking Luke's dad was going to get both barrels when I asked, "What would you like to say to your dad, Luke?"

I love you, Dad.

What? Really? You know, Luke, you can say any-thing . . . anything.

I did.

Thirteen-year-old Carrie spoke from the heart:

My dad is so frustrating.

Uh-huh, anything else Carrie?

I want to tell you, Dad, how much I love you.

Whew! That's a relief for us dads who frustrate our kids.

Thirteen-year-old Mary spoke of love even though her dad hurt her as a child:

You're the biggest, meanest, self-centered jerk. I hate you for what you did . . . but I love you.

Mary needs her dad to say, "I'm sorry." But that may never come her way. She loves him anyway; she's resilient.

Thirteen-year-old Andrea has also experienced childhood pain with her dad.

He is a selfish jerk who rates a 0 in my book, she wrote. *I have not seen him since I was two years old, and he was never there for me. I really hate him for that.*

Any words to your dad directly, Andrea?

I hate you, and I love you.

As you can see, kids have shared some really strong feelings and thoughts with me. Yet in this sample survey of 330 young people where nearly half used the word *love* toward their dads, only 2.1 percent used the word *hate.* Two of the ones who used the word *hate*—Mary and Andrea— also used the word *love* as the other half of their message. *I love you* is a central message coming to us dads from our kids.

THE VALUE OF LOVE

These kids' comments are what I call right-brain aspects of the *I love you* message, the emotional/interpersonal aspects of the message. In contrast, let me shift over to the left brain to get what some of us men like to see: the bottom-line numbers. Here is a detailed review of that test sample of 330 young people and how they dealt with the topic of love.

On the scale of one to ten, 75 percent rated their dads as six or higher. Only 23 percent rated their dads five or lower. The following graph shows the percentages of kids who gave their dads each rating:

I discovered an interesting trend when I analyzed the use of the word *love* in this sample. The higher the dad was rated on the one-to-ten scale, the more likely the young person used the word *love* in his or her comments:

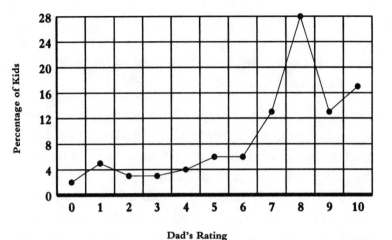

Percentage of Kids

Dad's Rating

- 55 percent of those who rated the relationship six or higher used the word *love*.
- Only 34 percent of those who rated the relationship five or lower used the word *love*.

Those percentages changed as the ratings went higher:

- 61 percent of those who rated their dads eight or higher used the word *love*.

And what about the dads who rated a ten?

- 73.7 percent of the kids who rated their dads a ten used the word love in their comments.

More than seven out of every ten kids who labeled their relationship with their dads a ten used the word *love* to describe that relationship and/or what they wanted to say to their dads. *Seven out of ten!*

How much did the percentage drop on the lower-rated relationships?

- Only 22.7 percent, roughly one out of every five young people who rated their dad a three or lower, used the word *love*.

Yet four kids who gave Dad a one also used the word *love*. When I investigated further I realized that two of those four had lost their dads to death, so they had no way to improve the rating of the relationship. Yet they still loved him.

Now I was really intrigued. Could this large sample be skewed or carry a margin of error? I decided to take the same approach to *all* fifteen hundred of the surveys, not just to this test sample. Are you ready?

- 70.1 percent of the kids who rated their dads as tens also used the word *love* in their comments.
- 57.8 percent of the kids ranking 8 or higher for Dad used *love*.
- 18 percent of the kids rating Dad three or lower used *love*.

The numbers stayed true. Love brings value to a relationship between Dad and child. Now let's look at some of the ways kids said they feel our love.

THE BUILDERS OF LOVE

The kids mentioned two ways they want us to let them know we love them:

- Show it.
- Say it.

That's it. Straightforward and simple. The kids spoke. I listened. Now I'm telling you what they said.

Show Them Your Love

Saint Francis of Assisi, a Christian monk from the Middle Ages whose life and words have inspired thousands, said, "Go and preach the gospel, and if you must, use words."

Let me adapt that wise man's words to fit our relationships with our kids: Go and love your kids, and if you must, use words.

Don't try to persuade your kids that you love them, prove it. Remove all doubt by letting your child see your love up close and personal. What is the best way to show your love for your child? We adults probably could come up with a hundred good ways, but let me again turn to the kids for their answers:

Ashley is fourteen. She thinks of *blue* when she thinks of her dad because blue is his favorite color. Does this teenager have anything to say to her dad?

I love you . . . and let's go fishing. Here's a girl who wants to spend the day cramped in a small boat out in the middle of who-knows-where in the hot sun with smelly fish and slimy bait! Surely, there is a mall to be roamed, some hair to be combed, or music to be droned. But not for Ashley. Being with Dad is a great place to be.

Gregg's dad is very important to him. He said,

My dad helps me in sports; we wrestle and spend time with each other.

Anything you want to say to Dad, Gregg?

I love you and thank you for spending time with me.

Later, when we talk about the *Be with me* message in Chapter 6, we'll explore in more detail what kids are saying about ways dads connect with their kids. For now, let me offer just one word to summarize what kids need from us to feel our love for them: *time*. That's it. To a kid, time is the most precious commodity. Somewhere in adolescence many kids adjust their economy of value from time to include money and power, but the predominant love-builder for a child is Dad's time. Bottom line, dads? Show your child he or she is loved *by being there.*

The second way to build love between a dad and a child is to employ what I consider to be the most powerful phrase in the language of humankind, and it's only three words long. I'll bet you've already guessed it: *I love you.* And don't just say it. Act it. Write it. Videotape it. Do whatever you need to do to get this phrase out to your child.

Tell Them of Your Love

During the past five years I have challenged literally thousands and thousands of young people to do what might have been the most difficult step some of them would ever face. I've urged them, "Tell your parents you love them."

I empathized with them by acknowledging that this might feel like an insurmountable challenge. Then I asked them the question I mentioned earlier: "Why does it seem so easy to say, 'I love you' to someone you just started dating, and yet you choke on those words when sharing them with Mom or Dad or another family member?"

The kids didn't have the answer, but a large portion of them usually nodded in agreement.

A high school student named Cappy wrote to let me know what happened after I challenged her and three hundred other students to go home and tell their moms and/or dads, "I love you." Here's what she had to say:

One thing that really got me thinking was when you said to go home and give our parents a hug and say, "I love you." Your interpretation of what they would do was exactly what I would've expected in my house. At the time I said to myself, "No way! My parents would freak." On Thursday I got up the courage to say it to my mom. She was cooking dinner and I went up to her and gave her a hug, and said, "I love you." Then I started to cry. I can't remember the last time I said that to her. She didn't understand, but she didn't ask any questions. I think I really made her night . . . week . . . month. I just wanted to thank you!

I've read Cappy's letter many times before, but I just noticed something for the first time when I included it in this chapter. She spoke of her parents in plural, but she never told me what happened with her dad. Who knows? I just hope she didn't leave him out because she could not muster the additional courage to tell him she loved him.

A popular music group, Mike and the Mechanics, brought the power of connecting with a dad to their hit song, "In the Living Years." In the song, a man describes how each generation passes fault on to the previous generation. He tells how he feels like a prisoner to his father's ways, his fears, his hopes. The listener can feel the tension and lingering conflict that remained over the years between the dad and his child.

In the next verse the son grieves his absence at his father's passing, how he left so many things unsaid, how he thinks he hears his father's voice in the cries of his newborn child. The final, powerful line of the chorus states, "I just wish I could have told him in the living years."[1]

Is it too late for your own relationship with your dad? I encourage you to say it anyway. Write your dad a letter, even if he is absent through death, divorce, or desertion. He may not hear you, but it will be an important step in your growth as well as in the relationship between you and your own child. Don't let that haunting song be the cry of your child's heart after you are gone. Speak the three most powerful words known—I love you.

Dad, are you ready? It's time to break the pattern. More kids have said these words since I challenged them. I'll finish the chapter as I began, letting the kids speak. All these kids want to say to Dad, "I love you":

Aaron	Angie	Candice	Dawn
Aimee	Artesja	Cecilia	Diana
Alexis	Ashleigh	Charles	Drew
Allison	Becky	Chris	Dustin
Alyssa	Ben	Christina	Elain
Amanda	Brandy	Christine	Elayna
Amber	Brian	Crystal	Elysia
Amy	Brooke	Dana	Erik
Andy	Cameron	Darla	Erika

Erin	Kathryne	Megan	Samuel
Faith	Kela	Melissa	Sarah
Frank	Kelly	Michael	Scott
Garret	Kenny	Michelle	Shawn
Geneva	Kevin	Mike	Shellie
Gerry	Kimberley	Mishel	Sherrie
Heather	Kristin	Naomi	Stacy
Holly	Laura	Natalie	Stephanie
Jeannine	Lauren	Nathan	Steven
Jennifer	Leah	Neal	Tara
Jessica	Lee	Nick	Tawny
Jillian	Lindy	Nicole	Teresa
Joana	Lisa	Paul	Tim
John	Lori	Peter	Tina
Jonathan	Mandy	Priscilla	Tobias
Joshua	Marisol	Ralph	Vanessa
Julius	Marlene	Randy	Vonetta
Kaitlin	Mary	Robert	William
Karrie	Matt	Ryan	Zabrina

Can you find your child's name? The list won't be complete without it.

Dear Dad,

   I love you. That's the most important message you could ever hear from me. Sometimes it is tough or awkward to say, but it's true—I love you.

Love,
Your child

CHAPTER 3

Dear Dad,

Please accept me.

Love,
Your child

PLEASE ACCEPT ME.

I appreciate my dad and how hard he tries to understand me.
Jan, age sixteen

I love you and hope to get past the barrier between us. Love me, not what you want me to be.
Vanessa, age seventeen

Do you accept me? Do you accept me for who I am, not for who I can or should be, or who you want me to be? Do you accept ME?
Roberto, age seventeen

I stood on the sidelines watching the young people organize a pickup game of basketball. A dozen coed students were lined up, ready to play.

The kids were familiar with schoolyard mores, so they picked two captains and let these more talented players choose their teams.

"I'll take Ryan," the first captain said. Ryan was small but fast, a sure bet for three-pointers.

"I'll take Mark," the other captain said. Mark was a boy past the threshold of puberty.

"I'll take Amelia." She was an amazing ball handler ("for a girl" they'd say) and a good shot.

"I'll take . . ." The verbal volley went back and forth until only two players were left.

The next-to-last player chosen was a female. She was tall

and lanky but rough with her ball handling. Honestly, I was impressed to see that she wanted to play.

That left just one player. If you've ever played a game of playground ball, you've surely seen this scenario. I was fortunate to have fair athletic skills, so I never faced what I saw so many last-pick guys go through. This time it was Justin who stood alone as the one no one wanted as a teammate.

"Go ahead you guys, take Justin," the first captain said.

"No, that's OK. You take him," replied the second. "We've got enough players."

Justin bounced back and forth like a ping-pong ball in tournament play.

Finally the first captain said, "OK, we'll take him." He turned to Justin and said, "Justin, you start on the sidelines and we'll call you in."

I watched Justin shuffle over to the sidelines with his head hanging low. I had played a game with Justin earlier, and his skills were really OK but his mouth couldn't hit the target. He made sure every other player knew what mistakes he or she made. His verbal defense was better than his game defense. In short, Justin was obnoxious.

I've seen it a dozen times: Some kid doesn't fit in or doesn't measure up, so he or she is left standing on the sidelines, desperately wanting to play, desperately asking one question: *Can I be on the team?*

Dad, in a world of brutal cuts, you're the head coach. Nobody—and I repeat, *nobody*—has the influence over your kid that you do. More important than making the team, the Justins of the world want to know that they have a "position" on your team. That's where the second of the eleven key messages of your kid's heart originates. They're saying, *Dad, please accept me.*

Listen to the kids:

Esther is thirteen, and she's hoping life with Dad will improve. She told me her relationship with her dad is a three. Why?

We don't ever get along. . . . He yells a lot, Esther said. Anger puts an obstacle between father and child. I asked what she would say if she could say anything to her dad. Esther replied,

Be my friend.

Here is a young girl who desperately wants her dad to be nothing more than a friend, someone who accepts her for who she is. A friend picks you to be on his team. A friend cheers for you whether you are winning or losing. Esther wants to look to the stands and see her dad waving her pennant.

Do young people really expect to come in two hours late for curfew and anticipate a dad's response to be, "That's OK. I accept you for who you are, not what you do"? Even kids are not that naive! But when it comes to the heart, they want pure acceptance, to know they belong. Separate your child's actions from who he or she is as your child, then you can always make him or her a member of the team regardless of the season's outcome. Can your son or daughter bat .219 and still make the cut?

In my time with kids, I have found some kids like Karine, Ronda, and Marcus, who are rejected to the core. Karine is seventeen and says her dad is a blue because,

It is a cold color, and he is very cold.

She told me what she really wanted her dad to hear was,

You may not like the fact that I'm here, but I'm here, and you need to accept that fact.

Why, Karine? What makes you think you are not accepted?

You love your stepchildren more than me.

Karine is not alone. Ronda is only twelve, but she has already faced an obstacle that may never be overcome. She gave her dad the color brown because, she wrote,

He loses his temper easy and cusses a lot.

Another mad dad. (In the next chapter, we'll take a close look at anger as an obstacle between father and child.) Her time with her dad, a valuable commodity for kids, is almost nonexistent. She said,

My parents are divorced and I don't see my dad very often, and when I do we don't do anything.

Ronda, if you could say anything, what would you say to your dad?

Why did you want to have an abortion with me?

Where did Ronda get the idea her dad wished to abort her? What does her dad have to say about it? Questions like these will go unanswered. Yet Ronda believes this is true, and her dad is doing little to show her otherwise.

I figured she was an isolated case. Then I came across Marcus. Although he's only twelve, he's got some strong feelings toward his dad. Listen to him:

My dad is the color black because he is never there for me. My relationship with him is a zero.

Why, Marcus?

My dad wanted me aborted.

I almost hate to ask. Marcus, do you have anything to say to your dad?

Go die because you've never been there for any of your children.

Again, the ultimate rejection.

One girl chose not to give me her name or age, just the message of her heart. She said,

He's the color black. He's like a black hole; never understanding or there. Our relationship is a one because he didn't want a girl, and he disowned me because of it.

Any comments to your dad?

I'm doing just fine without you.

I find her comment hard to believe. Young people are crying out for acceptance. As if hungry for the next meal, a relationally starved child will leave home in search of emotional nourishment. Often children choose destructive means—we in the kid business call it "acting out." They are looking for love and acceptance wherever they can get it. I put it this way: Young people will take on the values of those who consider them valuable.

Take gangs, for example. The allure is exciting, tempting, and dangerous. Ask any citizen of the largest cities across the United States today, and you will find "gangs and crime" on the top of his or her list of worries. In a recent survey, 19 percent of the people polled rated crime as the number-one problem facing the country today. The number-one problem! The research states that close to one-fifth of crime is committed by those younger than eighteen . . . kids! What would you guess is the peak of a typical crime career? Ages fifteen through twenty-three. Kids![1]

What did people rank as the second problem? Twelve percent said lack of morals/values. Do you see the key word buried in the response? *Value.* As I mentioned earlier, kids want us to accept them for who they are, not what they do.

What makes gangs so powerful? One word: *acceptance.* When a kid joins a gang, he or she is part of the team. What makes kids so vulnerable to the power of a gang's acceptance? *Dad's missing acceptance.*

Find an adult working with urban youth and ask, "What is the number-one reason for the breakdown of the family and the buildup of gangs?" and you will hear one primary answer: the missing dad. "Kids without fathers are forced to find their own ways of doing things. So they come up with their own ideas from friends and from the gangs. Nobody is showing them what to do except to be drunk, deal drugs, or go to jail," states Melissa Manning, a social worker at the Boys and Girls Club of Venice, California.[2]

Listen again to the young people who face gangs on a daily basis.

Diego: "People join gangs for protection, to stand out, to have friends."

Anthony: "Kids who don't get no attention at school join gangs to get attention. That's the worst thing about school, the gangs."[3]

Where do these precious young boys find the acceptance they desperately need from Dad? A child lacking acceptance from his or her dad is wide open to destructive behaviors and/or people who will bring acceptance. Remember, kids take on the values of those who consider them valuable. With an empty spot for love and acceptance, the young person is driven to fill the void. The cost to the child seeking acceptance is secondary to the benefit of belonging. Find me a young girl lacking her father's acceptance, and I will show you a female on the threshold of sexual promiscuity and teenage pregnancy.

Dad, you hold the key. You and I matter. We fathers possess the most powerful position on the earth. With the investment of paternal acceptance, we can literally change the face of our globe's social landscape. If you're feeling guilty right now, it may be appropriate. Face the facts. Do you find rebellion in the kingdom? If you ask your child what he or she thinks about you and the response is filled with ugly colors, low numbers, and disheartening comments, listen up!

I am not striving to leave a pile of fathers stacked in a heap of guilt. We've got enough pain and despair in our world. Go back to this book's original discovery: You and I matter, possibly more than we will ever realize.

Listen to the kids again.

Corrine, a sixteen-year-old girl, gives dad the color pink because

He catches the eye of everyone and holds their attention.

Corrine, on a scale of one to ten, where does your relationship with Dad stand?

Definitely a ten! He's my best friend, and his opinions I value the most.

Final words directly to your dad, Corrine?

What an influence you have had on and in my life.

Corrine is not unique. You are in possession of a leverage capable of lifting your child higher than you can fathom.

Don't let your pride worry about the size of the lever. Don't concentrate on the position of the fulcrum. Every moment you wait moves the fulcrum closer to you and farther from your child. You know what happens? It takes more to lift the same amount of weight. Don't analyze, Dad. Don't talk about what you could have, should have, or would have done. Instead put all your might into the lever, and watch your child soar.

Are you ready to ask where to put your power for the best leverage? Let me offer a few key points of contact I have heard from young people.

INVEST VALUE INTO YOUR CHILD

One of my favorite stories is about a management meeting that took place in a dog-food company. The president looked out to his company's key leaders and asked, "Who has the best sales force in the business?"

"We do," they responded.

"Who has the best marketing campaign?"

"We do."

"Who has the best customer service in the industry?"

"We do."

"Now then," the president continued, "who has the worst sales of all dog-food brands?"

"We do" the group responded.

"Why?" the president demanded.

From the back of the conference room came the sheepish rise of a hand then these words, "'Cause the dogs won't eat the food."

Let's face it. If you are in the dog-food business and your

main constituent does not consume your product, you are destined for the corporate doghouse!

I don't mean to equate kids with dogs. Dogs are easier to train. Kids are kids, thank God. Still, I want you to ask yourself, "What do my kids value from me?" Better yet, stay with the approach of this book. Ask your kids, "What is the best way for me to let you know I accept you for who you are?"

I can't tell you exactly what your child may consider important. Corrine spoke positively about her dad, but it was in generalities. Your challenge is to find the currency that is most valuable to your child, the consumer. I've gleaned some insight from Stephen Covey, who talks about an emotional bank account when he describes a person's relational value system.

What is an emotional bank account? It comes from the amount of trust you have invested in a relationship. Covey has helped me learn that these actions and values in a relationship make deposits in the emotional bank account:

- Understanding
- Attention
- Promise keeping
- Clear expectations
- Integrity
- Sincere apologies[4]

It is our challenge as dads to adjust, reorder, add, or delete from this list to meet our children's needs. It is highly likely that those of us who have more than one offspring need to redo our responses for each child. Even a rebellious son or daughter can still be within reach. "Rebellion is a knot of the heart, not of the mind," wrote Covey.[5]

In their best-selling book, *The 22 Immutable Laws of Marketing,* Al Reis and Jack Trout bring this same principle into the world of business. Basically, they say you can't change a perception. You can only match your product or service to the corresponding need.6 Funny how this principle of good business corresponds with wise fathering. I am convinced most truly successful businessmen would thrive as dads (if they don't already) by applying the principles of effective business leadership at home. More accurately, effective dads turn out to be good workers, managers, and leaders.

One of history's most prolific authors, the apostle Paul, places the priority of leadership in the correct order in reference to the church: "If a man does not know how to rule his own house, how will he take care of the church of God?"[7] This same wisdom applies to every institution of our society.

A dad's most effective means of communicating acceptance to his child is to invest value into his child. The value-added approach is the best "rebellion-proof" method. It is also the most guaranteed way to pass on your family values to your child, for kids take on the values of those who consider them valuable. What's in store for your child's interpersonal inheritance? And, equally important, who is helping you raise your son or daughter?

WHO IS HELPING YOU RAISE YOUR KIDS?

I sat in a parenting seminar nearly ten years ago listening to Jim Slevcove, a man who has dedicated his life to kids—first to his own three children who are now adults, and then to thousands of others as a board member of colleges and camps and as the founder of his own camp. This sage man asked a poignant question: "Who is helping you raise your kids?"

I immediately noticed his assumption: Kids are not meant to be raised by parents alone. Someone else is going to influence your kids whether it's by design or default. Relatives, church leaders, teachers, MTV, movies, peers. Your role is not a solo run.

I have spent my career as one of those someone elses, as a "paraparent" who walks alongside the family. (There is no mistake in the affinity between a paraparent and paramedic; both are called to the scene of an accident to help the injured survive.) The last five years of my professional investment in kids and families have been through the National Institute of Youth Ministry. The organization was begun in 1985 by my friend and colleague Jim Burns, who has grown to be one of the most respected voices for youth in the country today.

Driving the dream of the National Institute of Youth Ministry is a twofold motive: First, families need support. It is very difficult to raise a child today. We exist to help. Second, the most strategic way to reach as many young people as possible is to assist the adults who work and live with these kids—the parents, pastors, coaches, teachers, scout leaders, and other volunteers or professionals committed to today's kids. Our board members like to call it "leverage." In my journey with NIYM and in the decade prior to my joining the ministry, I have confirmed the powerful influence of a well-partnered adult on the life of a child. Again, we adults matter. And Dad, you lead the parade.

A team of researchers headed by Frances Ianni of Columbia University's Teachers College observed adolescents in ten communities over the past ten years. Ianni stated, "We much more hear teenagers preface comments to their peers with 'my mom says' than with any attributions to heroes of the youth culture."[8]

Yet this changes somewhat when there's turmoil and social change. Dr. John Schowalter, president of the American Academy of Child and Adolescent Psychiatry, says teenagers have a tendency to break loose and follow each other more at those times. "The leadership of adults is somewhat splintered and they're more on their own sort of like *Lord of the Flies*," he said.[9]

Do all kids want to break loose from adult influence during their teenage years? No way! Ruby Takanishi, director of the Carnegie Council on Adolescent Development, said, "The society is still permeated by the notion that adolescents are different, that their hormones are raging around and they don't want to have anything to do with their parents or other adults."[10]

It's not true, insisted Takanishi. There have been studies on what is called "invulnerable adolescents," young people who became functioning adults in spite of their possibly troubled upbringing. As Frances Ianni said, "A lot of people have attributed this to some inner resilience. But what we've seen in practically all cases is some caring adult figure who was a constant in that kid's life."[11]

Dr. David Carson, a consultant with the National Institute of Mental Health, reinforced the power of a caring adult when he was asked the question, "How does the young person make it through?" He replied:

Think of the African American male. Some think the only way a young black male can get out of the ghetto is to play professional sports. But if you want to get out of the economically depressing culture of the ghetto, statistically the best chance is to go to church. Statistics show that those young black males who get out of the ghetto are church attenders. And by the way, they are also the people who, if they keep their religion, are most likely to come back to the ghetto and try to change things.[12]

Dr. Carson's insights are echoed across the nation. "In many neighborhoods, the black church has led the awakening."[13] The same is true from what I have seen across the world in various cultures, races, and economic groups. What does a young person, regardless of race and social status, find in the church?

- *Value-centered living.* Healthy behavior guidelines based on a historic, moral way of living that was mutually agreed upon by an entire community.
- *Positive, hopeful attitudes.* A resurrection faith that believes obstacles—with the sting of death or the weight of a rock seemingly too big to roll away—can be overcome. The parking brake can be released.
- *Loving, dedicated adults.* Here are caring people, who model their lives after other persons past and present. In my business, we call these caring adults "youth

workers," adults who care enough to walk alongside a young person and his or her family to provide the acceptance, affirmation, and challenge for the child to become an "invulnerable adolescent."

- *The power of the Other.* The love, acceptance, and grace of a God who sought out His people throughout the course of history and remains active and alive today.

I heard a volunteer youth worker tell Rich Van Pelt, one of our nation's experts in teenage crisis and also the director of Alongside, an organization for youth, "I'm not trained in these issues. How could I ever help a young person in crisis?"

Rich, author of *Intensive Care,* replied, "Teenagers who survive crisis do so because they have a caring adult who remained constant in their life."

Rich would never place a child in major crisis in the hands of an untrained adult, but his point underscored the power of a constant, caring adult to provide acceptance to a child in need. That is the common denominator among kids who make it through.

Two dads in Atlanta have recognized that power. Bob Crowder, an attorney and father of four, and Derwin Brown, a police lieutenant, began the Fathers Foundation to help black men raise their children. Brown grew up without a dad but found other men who were valuable role models. He said, "They always called you son." The two dads don't have fairy-tale dreams of their impact; they just want to stand alongside some other warriors battling for the good of our kids.[14]

Dad, who is helping you raise your kids? Who is helping

you invest value into your child and build your child's emotional bank account? I urge you to seek out some partners in the role of being a dad. Let me offer a few:

- *Your local church.* Call around to neighborhood churches and inquire about their ministry to young people. Find one that wants to partner with you and take it up on its offer. Get the name of a parent in the church who respects and appreciates what is happening, then call for his or her opinion. I'm willing to venture that you'll get good stuff, and most of it will be free. Studies across the nation support this advice.

- *Your peers.* For the last five years, I have gathered weekly to meet with four other guys. As fathers of twelve kids cumulatively, we've banded together to help each other learn and grow as dads (and husbands, as well as other roles). These friends have become my partners, supporters, coaches, drill sergeants, and avid fans. I recommend that you find an existing group and crash in. Or start one of your own if you need to. It's well worth the time and energy. I'll give you the names of four references if you need proof.

- *Your child's school.* I wonder why we dads sometimes give more consideration to our car mechanic than to our children's teachers. Set up an appointment with your child's teacher. Use this time to build the teacher's emotional bank account, gain advice on your child's participation in school, and offer whatever support you can. Every teacher I know is underpaid and over-worked yet truly committed to our kids' well-being.

- *Your child's friends and their families.* One of the most exciting movements across our nation has been the creation of adult-sponsored, drug- and alcohol-free graduation-night parties for kids. They began when some parents pooled their love, creativity, and resources to give their graduating seniors a better party than they could ever find on their own. The good news is that kids will live to tell about these parties with less risk of alcohol- or drug-related accidents, the greatest killer of today's young people.
- *Other organizations committed to parenting.* See page 238 for a valuable list of parenting resources available to dads.

MAKING THE TEAM CAN HAPPEN EARLY OR LATE

Scott McCorkle, a former high school star at Capistrano Valley High School in my area of southern California, played basketball with Syracuse University. As he played an outstanding game one night against the University of Pittsburgh in the winter of 1994, ESPN analyst Dick Vitale embellished the moment with his dynamic color commentary, saying, "It may be freezing outside, but he's on fire."

What drove Scott to reach new heights and finish the game with thirteen points and six rebounds? One word: *Dad.* "I picked him out before the game," Scott said. "Every time I did something, I looked up in the stands. He was clapping, smiling, just having a really good time."

That night was the first time Ray Lundeen, Scott's dad, had watched his son play for Syracuse. Every time Scott would score, he would point to his dad in the stands. "Having him there, seeing his approval, meant so much to me," Scott said.

Scott's parents divorced when he was six years old. His mother remarried, and Scott took on the name of his stepfather, Doug McCorkle. Scott would visit his father periodically, and his dad was able to see some of his high school basketball games.

Scott reconnected with his dad as a college freshman when he followed the advice of his grandmother to start writing to his dad. His dad was able to visit Scott a few times at college, but he never saw him play in person.

Scott said, "Every year, I would invite him to a game. The beginning of each season, I'd send him a schedule. But he was always busy."

Something blocked their relationship. Scott wondered if it stemmed from his changing his name from Lundeen to McCorkle. His dad admitted, "There were things I don't want to talk about, family issues. The name was part of it. But part of it was I didn't have an opportunity to get down there."

Yet in 1994 Scott's dad came for a five-day visit that included two games. "We had a lot of catching up to do," Scott said. Father and son were on the road to reconnecting.

Scott McCorkle had a great season with a career high of eighteen points against Villanova. As good as that game was, the night when Syracuse played against Pittsburgh in the winter of '94 warms his heart the most. He said it was the most fun he'd had in a game since he played at Capistrano Valley High.

Scott was so fired up he ran by announcer Dick Vitale and shouted, "Oh baby, give me the ball!"

Vitale said, "He's got the three *E*s. He's exciting, he has energy, and he has enthusiasm. . . . Don't worry, Scotty, we're giving you some PR."

Scott McCorkle was not looking for PR. He did not need the cheerleading. His most important fan was already in the stands.

His dad said, "He made a jumper from the side, then circled up court and pointed at me. The people around me picked up on that. They asked me, 'Do you know him?' I said, 'Yeah, that's my son.'"[15]

Yeah, that's my son. He's on my team. He made the cut. I'm cheering for him until the game's over, win or lose. The positive role models always seem to use those phrases, and they can get away with it.

So far, this is what we've heard from the kids:

Dad, you matter to me.

Dad, I love you, still and in spite of who you are sometimes.

Dad, does your child know that he or she belongs to you? Does he or she have a starting position on your team? Your acceptance will make or break your child.

Dear Dad,

Dad, please accept me.
Do I matter to you?
Unless I know I matter to
you, who you are and what
you say will matter less and
less to me. My heart cries for
you, but my life will rebel if
my message goes unheard.

With love,
Your child

CHAPTER 4

Dear Dad,

Please don't hurt me.

Love,
Your child

PLEASE DON'T HURT ME.

Dad [a stepdad and father number three for this young man], *why? Why did you have an affair? Why did you do this to me? Why are you hurting us? I have more questions than statements.*
John, age sixteen

My dad is like the color red . . . he's always angry. If I could say anything to my dad I'd say, You don't know how much you hurt me.
Yvonne, age fourteen

I'm always afraid of him . . . he doesn't know how much he hurts me when he's done the things he's done.
Rayleen, age sixteen

Jamie, my middle daughter, is very affectionate in both her words and actions. She often looks up at me, bats her big brown eyes, reaches up with both arms, smiles that heart-melting smile, and says, "Uppie, Daddy, uppie."

Who could say no?

Yet sometimes Jamie's desire to be held outpaces my holding supply. I'd love to say otherwise, but I've got to be honest. One day I left the office early to watch the kids while my wife took care of some business. In tag-team style, I arrived at home and she took off, leaving Mr. Mom in charge. It's a role I value and practice often, but on this particular day I still had some unfinished business at work, so I grabbed our cordless phone, took off for a quiet corner of the house, and began my calls.

Jamie, however, was ready for me to focus on her—and Jamie has tremendous persistence. She'll follow and ask, ask and follow, trail and talk, talk and trail. That day she trailed me like a puppy, whining, "Daddy, uppie, Daddy, uppie, Daddy, uppie, Daddddddddyyyyyy, upppppieeeee, Dadddddddddddyyyyyy . . ."

I tried to be polite; really I did. I offered a few *Not right now*'s and a couple of *Jamers, when I'm done talking on the phone*'s. But I ran out of patience before she ran out of persistence. What followed was not pretty.

I clearly remember walking into a room with Jamie right on my heals, howling, "Daddy, uppie, Daddy . . ." I said good-bye on the phone, turned it off, pushed down the antenna, spun around, and let out a yell:

"SHUUUTTTT UUPPPPP!"

The room went deathly silent. Jamie was momentarily shocked. I was too. She dropped her blanket, and her bottom lip began to shake. Her cry was short-circuited for a moment, then she started to wail and quickly darted downstairs to her room. I looked up to see Jamie's big sister, our oldest daughter, Brookelyn. She, too, was stunned and on the verge of tears. She had never seen Daddy react like that before.

"I'm sorry . . . I'm sorry, Brookelyn. Daddy was wrong. I've got to talk to Jamie."

When I got to Jamie's room, she was curled up on her bed, crying, shaking, and desperately clinging to her only stronghold, her pillow.

"Jamie," I stuttered, "I'm sorry. You did not deserve that.

That was a terrible way for Daddy to talk to you. I'm really sorry. Will you forgive me?"

By that time she was in my arms, sobbing and gasping. I cuddled her for a few moments until she calmed down. "I'm sorry, sweetie," I repeated ever so gently.

"That's OK, Daddy. I forgive you." Jamie then looked up at me and said, as though she were now the parent and I the scolded child, "Daddy, you said 'shut up.' We're not supposed to say that. It's not nice to say that."

Not only did I hurt my dear child, I broke a family rule. Nice fathering, eh?

This chapter is a tough one. Let's admit it. You and I would just as soon skip this one. Or you may be thinking, "I'm glad this is not an issue for me. My kids mean too much to me to hurt them."

I know how you feel. You've already read how much my kids mean to me. I have such a deep love for them, the last thing I want to do is hurt them. Yet I can't say that I am writing this chapter as an outside observer.

Once you and I realize how much we really matter to our kids, we can very easily discern that our words and actions can really hurt. I find too many kids with one plea to their dads: *Please don't hurt me.*

I'd like to introduce you to a few of those kids.

A COLORFUL PERSPECTIVE

As you know by now, one of the questions I've put in front of hundreds of children is: "If you were to describe your dad with a color, what would he be?"

It's a simple, easy-to-answer question, and it's subjective

so it opens up the heart. The kids' responses? Green, lots of blue, yellow, pink, white, even obscure colors, as you'll read in the Epiphany section of *Dear Dad*. I've also received a few responses that mentioned unusual colors, like fourteen-year-old Katrina's choice. She chose maroon and used it to describe her dad this way:

He is moody when it comes to some things. . . . Well, okay, he's moody when it comes to most things.

Seventeen-year-old Vanessa had a completely different thought in mind when she selected the color khaki to paint her dad.

He's very stern and solid, but he's also a dork. . . . We're exactly the same.

My dad's a dork—just like me! Kind of endearing, isn't it? I wish all kids were as encouraging and lighthearted as Vanessa. I've found too many kids who feel otherwise.

Fifteen percent chose the color red to portray their dad. Why red? Some kids used red to describe a caring, loving dad:

It's my heart.
Kristi, age twelve

He always jokes around and is laughing and turns red.
Roxanne, age thirteen

Strong and caring.
Steven, age thirteen

He's awesome.
Matthew, age thirteen

Other kids chose the color for a combination of opposite reasons:

> *He turns red when he's happy and mad.*
> Christine, age fourteen

> *He's bright and happy, but he gets mad a lot.*
> Miranda, age fourteen

Still others used red to paint a real fire. Forty-nine percent of them chose the color to describe their dad's anger:

> *He's a very angry and violent person.*
> Anonymous female, age sixteen

> *He has a temper.*
> Shawna, age seventeen

> *Because he is really mad (all the time).*
> Carl, age twelve

Analyzing the kids' responses, I gained a strong, profound insight: There's a surplus of mad dads. For some kids, the color red didn't say enough. Fifteen-year-old Marta needed something stronger. She chose black, as 10 percent of the kids did. Why black? Here's what Marta said:

He really doesn't care for us. I'd like to have a dad that would care for me . . . not just yelling and being mean to me.

As you can imagine, black conjured up a certain image with most of the kids who chose it. (Not all picked black for negative reasons, however; 16.9 percent of those who chose the color black did so for a positive or neutral reason. A few have African-American dads, so they selected the color of his skin.) A thirteen- and twelve-year-old both chose black for these reasons:

He's mean and angry.

He's mean and scary. I don't want to know him.

Thirteen-year-old Arthur decided that neither red nor black said enough alone, so he picked them both. Why?

He is angry almost all the time, Arthur wrote.

What would Arthur say if he could say anything to his dad?

Why can't you be nice to me?

I wonder what Arthur's dad would say if he could hear his boy's plea? I'm afraid to think how that dad might respond. I can virtually guarantee you that one young teenager in the Northwest would rather be lonely than provoke a mad dad with his heartfelt request. Unfortunately, I find too many young people like Arthur.

One sixteen-year-old declined to give a name but took to the attack:

Our relationship will never grow because of your short temper . . . the way you become violent when things don't go your way.

A dear friend of mine recently shared with a group of us how he finds himself yelling so often at his fourteen-year-old son. He told us how he asked him, "Why do you not do what I ask until I yell? I don't like to have to yell to get your response." How did his son react? "Oh, Dad, that's OK. It doesn't mean that much when you yell."

Sometimes yelling doesn't bring results. Yet 10.2 percent of the kids used the words *anger, angry, temper,* or *mad* to describe their dads. Think of that: More than one out of ten kids is carrying feelings of anger from his or her relationship with Dad.

Another anonymous respondent implied that the deep, hurtful message was pushing him or her to the edge of death:

Dad, I wish you knew how much I'm hurting and want to give up on life.

With suicide being the third leading cause of death for young people ages fifteen to twenty-four and with the rates tripling in the past forty years, this nameless person is not alone.[1]

If you had the privilege to spend the time I do with kids, you would very quickly come to this conclusion: Many of today's young people are enraged. They're steaming hot. Why? I'm convinced it's partly because a lot of their dads are also really mad . . . enraged . . . steaming hot. Anger is everywhere we turn in our world. We're living in a country gone mad. We find anger in the media, in the workplace, on the streets, and definitely on the freeways here in Southern California.

Do you remember a few years back when we had a rash of freeway shootings around Los Angeles? Normal traffic transformed into vigilante commuting. Creative Southern California entrepreneurs came up with bumper stickers that said, "Don't shoot! I'll move over," or my favorite, "Cover me, I'm changing lanes." We even had window-suction message boards in the shape of a target. What a crazy place to live! Our world is full of people who are wound too tight. Sometimes it only takes a nudge to push a person over the edge.

For some of us dads, anger is blocking the way to our kids.

I have discovered three big barriers that choke the dad/child relationship. In short, Dad, you and I have to move our big *A*s out of the way:

Anger
Absence
Authority

Our focus now is on overcoming the first A: Anger, the primary barrier disconnecting a dad from his child. In Chapter 6 we will look at absence, which takes its toll when the child reaches the end of the monologue stage and transitions into the dialogue stage. Authority becomes a block when a child enters the epilogue stage in the mid- to late-teen years as dealt with in chapters 10 and 11, which focus on the *Trust me* and *Leave me alone* messages.

ANGER DISCONNECTS A FATHER FROM HIS CHILD

Two of the eleven kid-messages discussed in this book deal with anger: *Don't hurt me* and *Don't hurt you*. Allow me to highlight a few of the kids' comments on this topic:

Wade, a thirteen-year-old, colored his dad gray because, he wrote,

He has good sides and bad sides.

If Wade could say anything to his dad, he would offer,

I love you and wish you could improve your temper.

Wade gave his dad an eight. That's a top-notch rating for a kid who also said,

Sometimes we get in fights.

What keeps the rating from being higher? Wade believes the restraining force is his dad's anger.

Thirteen-year-old Douglas considers it fun to wrestle with his dad. The touch of a father is vitally important for an early-adolescent as he or she strives to develop into an adult. Wrestling is often a young boy's way of hugging without being uncool. But what happens when Douglas and Dad go at it?

My dad has a short temper.

What do you want to share with your dad from your heart, Douglas?

Try to not get mad so easily.

Imagine the scene: Dad comes in the house after a long day at work and all of a sudden, *Hhhiiiiiiyyyyyyyy-aaaaaahhhhhh!* Power Ranger Douglas strikes from behind the sofa. Dad goes down to his knees but quickly tosses his son off his back. In midflight, Douglas's foot catches Dad's briefcase and sends it flying.

As Douglas, a young boy with a truckload of testosterone, positions himself to pounce again on his weary victim, a collision of feelings is clanging around in his mind. *I can pin my dad, I know I can. At the same time, I love this man. I can't wait every day for him to get home. I wish he never had to leave for work.* The father/son relationship is soaring toward a record-high ten. Then the barrier-erecting words crash through, "|@%#$@★ it, Douglas! Now look at what you've done. That's my expensive briefcase with very important papers in it. How would you feel if I threw your school backpack into the street?"

Silence wraps the room in a headlock. Douglas's heart is

pinned to the mat. The father/son rating just plummeted to the ground. Dad's anger got in the way. Love was disconnected.

Few things will choke love faster than uncontrolled anger. In my own journey through life, I've discovered three profound insights about this emotion I believe we dads need to know: Anger is learned, anger is a secondary response, and anger is a choice.

Anger Is Learned

Until I was in my late twenties I thought I did not have any anger because I was outwardly a nice guy. Then I realized I had a milder version of anger that worked its way out in sarcasm or silence.

We learn how to be angry in the same way we learn how to ride a bike, manage money, or speak a language. We pick it up from our families, primarily our parents, and one of the primary legacies we dads pass on to our kids is how to handle anger. Sobering thought, isn't it? Too often I see kids acting out venomous anger they learned at home. Let me illustrate what I mean.

An article on the *Los Angeles Times* sports page caught my eye. The headline read: "Indiana Suspends Knight for Game." Bobby Knight, the well-known coach of the Indiana University Hoosiers basketball team, was suspended for one game because of his conduct in a game against Notre Dame. What triggered his anger, or should I say, what did Bobby choose to get angry at? The article states that Knight's outburst was triggered by some sloppy play in the closing minutes of the game by Hoosier reserves. (It's interesting to me that we traditionally use the word *trigger* in relation to anger, referring to the integral device on a weapon that unleashes the destructive force in the barrel: the bullet.)

What kind of sloppy play took place? Pat Knight, Bobby's son and a reserve for the Hoosiers, made a bad pass, which a Notre Dame player intercepted and took in for a layup. Okay, let's cut the older Knight some slack. In the heat of competition, it's easy to lose control, especially when the team could be in jeopardy of throwing the game away. What coach or athlete hasn't had a moment like that?

Yet take a second look at this situation. First, note the word *reserves*. The first string was out, and the bench was in. Indiana was up by twenty-eight points in the closing minutes of the game . . . twenty-eight points! The Hoosiers ended up winning by nineteen points, not exactly what you'd call a close game. So much for the threat-of-losing excuse!

The second interesting word in the story is *Knight,* and I don't mean Bobby. I'm referring to Pat Knight, son of the head coach. Apparently Bobby coached Pat a little too strongly when his son let the errant pass be intercepted. During the next time-out, Bobby screamed at his son as the players headed to the bench. Bobby kicked at something in anger, and some of the fans thought the coach was kicking his son. They began booing the coach.

Then the coach did what all angry coaches do to fans who support their teams and help pay their salaries. He stood up and glared at the crowd. I wonder if he used the same gesture that's so popular on our southern California freeways? If I had been in the crowd, I would have been ducking out of Bobby's way in case he chose to let another chair fly like he did back in 1985 when he erupted during a Hoosiers home game against Purdue.

Later, before the next game, Bobby read a statement to the crowd; he said he was deeply sorry and wished to apologize.

The story doesn't end there, however. Although Bobby Knight was ejected from that game, the night was still not without a Knight. True to the family colors, Pat Knight carried on the family tradition. During that next game he was ejected when he and a Tennessee Tech player went to the floor in a brawl in the second half of the game. Could it have been that a close game *triggered* Pat's response? I'm not sure what the score was when it happened, but we do know a reserve player was in, it was the second half, and Indiana ended up winning by forty-four points!

The Knights have reminded me that anger is passed on from father to son. I guess we can give Bobby the assist for that one. Too bad it wasn't intercepted before his son picked it up.

Anger is a learned behavior, and guess what, guys: Most kids take their coaching from Dad.

I've learned another insight about anger: Anger is a secondary response.

Anger Is a Secondary Response

It has helped me a great deal to know that anger is a secondary reaction to a preexisting feeling. Where does anger come from? Frustration, hurt, fear, and injustice. Keep enough of those primary feelings buried deep in your gut and *whammo!* A car's unexpected lane change, a bad pass, or a child's desire to be held will blow open the door of your soul. Anger is not primary; instead, it comes from those key prompters: frustration, hurt, fear, and injustice.

Frustration causes anger. Sometimes I get angry because I am frustrated that something or someone is not working as I had hoped. If I can't get the nut off a bolt, I get frustrated. If the kids mess up a room or part of the yard I just spent time cleaning, I get frustrated. If I'm stuck in traffic and I can't get where I'm trying to go—you got it, I'm frustrated. Basically, the majority of my frustration happens when my agenda is squashed.

Before I validate my anger, I've got to do a quick agenda check. Am I yelling at the kids because they did something wrong or because they inconvenienced me? Humbling consideration, isn't it, to think that my selfishness might be behind my frustration. Fourteen-year-old Katie was right when she said her dad *needs to think about other people too.*

Whether my agenda is good or bad, selfless or selfish, frustration is a very common precursor to anger. Hurts also trigger anger.

Hurt triggers anger. If Jamie were older, say a teenager, and I had yelled at her in the same way, she probably would have gotten extremely angry with me. Why? I had hurt her deeply. Why are so many kids angry? They are really hurting. They live in a world of shattered dreams and broken relationships. Of course, some of us dads like to say wise things like, "Oh, it doesn't hurt that bad." Or, "You'll get over it." Or worse yet, "You know, when I was your age

. . ." Then our kids just bury their hurts deeper and later find a stronger language of anger to let their souls speak out. These angry kids destroy lives, and they begin with their own.

Third, many people who are scared get very angry.

Fear sparks anger. Have you ever tried to wake up someone only to startle him or her unexpectedly and then experience the verbal or even physical wrath generated by his or her reaction to your efforts? I've heard about a young woman whose family dreaded trying to wake her up in the morning because of her strong and sometimes violent reaction. She'd get spooked and come up swinging and screaming.

How about the dad who waits up for his tardy teenager to come home late? What's racing through his mind? *I hope my kid is all right. What if something terrible has happened? What if he is hurt?* Panic, worry, and fear put a death-grip on Dad. Then the kid comes strolling in like it is the middle of a Saturday afternoon. With a sigh of relief, Dad blurts out, "I'm so glad you're OK. I was concerned that you may have been hurt. Now that you're home safe and sound, I think I'm going to kill you for being late!" Fear sends some people running, but others choose to fight. Fear is a strong motivator of anger, as is unjust treatment.

Injustice prompts anger. Wherever injustice exists in our world, anger is a close neighbor. Riots have rocked the city of Los Angeles because of the anger many local citizens have toward injustice in the community. People believe something's not right, and they are ticked off.

Since anger is a learned behavior, we can help our kids know when anger is appropriate. If something is bad enough to make you pound the table, it may be strong enough for you to take action to right the wrong. If a dad finds a child treating a sibling unjustly, anger may be appropriate. A lot of kids feel treated unjustly. I would not be surprised to find a teenager walking around the house with a T-shirt that proclaims, "NO JUSTICE . . . NO PEACE." I think Melinda, one of the kids who took the survey, might stand in line to buy that shirt and then wear it boldly. As a fifteen-year-old, she described her dad as red because

He has a bad temper and sometimes he blows up about the smallest thing. . . . If I ask something, he'll jump down my throat and say NO!

Where is the injustice? In Melinda's case, she believed her dad didn't respect her or listen to her. If you could only see her writing. She used a lot of uppercase letters, and as she moved down the page, these letters got bigger in size and were decorated with plenty of exclamation points that stood tall like soldiers in an army ready to do battle for her feelings. Her last words launched guerrilla warfare:

Next time, let me express my feelings. Because I have my problems to solve. You treat me like @%#$@^*. I can't even talk to you without you yelling your @%#$@^* head off about some dumb thing. So @%#$@^* you. Because YOU DON'T CARE!

It breaks my heart to think how Melinda will act out her anger over the next few years.

Cynda is another example. At "almost sixteen," Cynda wrote this about her dad:

My dad would be the color black because he is just like a black hole who sucks up everyone and spits them out.

My relationship with my dad would be a two because he thinks he is the world's greatest dad but he is just a blind fool.

As you can see from the kids' comments throughout this chapter, Melinda is not alone. I was truly shocked to see how much young people commented about their dads' anger. Apparently many, many dads are very angry, and their kids are unjustly hurt because of it.

The final powerful principle I've discovered is this: I choose to be angry.

Anger Is a Choice

I could have easily said to Jamie, "You make me so mad!" But heck, it kind of loses some punch if I look at my kid, clamp my jaw, and do one of those talk-through-my-teeth-without-opening-my-mouth scoldings, saying, "I'm choosing to be angry right now!" I know it's insightful, but it puts too much responsibility on me to be in charge of my own actions. It's much easier to blame Jamie for her lack of understanding of Daddy's busy schedule and heavy workload. Of course, when I blame I shame. And when I shame . . . I destroy.

Once I realized I could choose my emotional response, a whole new world opened up to me. I call it "adulthood." Anger is only the lead horse pulling a cart full of other feelings, and I'm learning to run the baggage through customs.

What can we dads do if we sense or hear our kids telling us directly, "Don't hurt me"? I offer two action steps that are helping me to describe my fathering with more *uuupppp-iiieee!* and less *SHUUUTTTT UUPPPPP!*

Check your weapons at the door. In the Old West, and possibly in parts of our world today, hotel clerks used to hang a sign above the door that read: CHECK YOUR WEAPONS AT THE DOOR. It was a safeguard against a run-of-the-mill conflict turning into a shootout. After all, shootouts at the OK Corral were one thing, but it would be quite messy if the hotel lobby were turned into a shooting gallery.

When I take my weapons from the day and swagger into my living room like it's high noon, I know my kids are going to get some buckshot they don't deserve. It's the same thing on the road. I'm convinced the guy on the freeway is delivering a message to me that needs to be aimed elsewhere—to his wife, his boss, or very possibly his dad. I just happened to be in the line of fire.

How do you and I check our guns at the door? Stephen Covey offers insights in his book *Seven Habits of Highly Effective People*. He said that as he pulls into his driveway after a day at work he reminds himself that he is about to start the most important work of his day. He lets go of his professional agenda and takes on the influential role of being a dad.[2]

What is a practical way to remind yourself to leave your weapon at the door so when your kids are doing what they do best—being kids—they won't flip your trigger? How about taking off your company security badge and hanging it on the rearview mirror? Or, what if you left your business card on your dashboard, then put it back in your wallet when you head for work? One guy calls his wife from the office or from his car each day before he arrives home. Consider picking a certain street on the way home to let your "worker" mind-set out of the car and let your "dad" role in. What a great way to make the transition from office to home.

The change comes when we learn to check our weapons at the door. And when our guns are holstered, what do we do next? It's time to wise up.

Be a wise guy, not a fool. I've picked up some insights from a book I highly recommend. It's a best-seller; frankly, it's *the* best-seller: the Bible. In the middle of the older section, the Old Testament, you can find a collection of wise sayings from one of history's longest-lasting civilizations. The Hebrew book of Proverbs is a book of wisdom. I call it "street smarts." If you are not familiar with it, you would probably recognize it by its best-known axiom—to paraphrase, "Spare the rod, spoil the child."[3] (Can you tell the book was written by a dad?)

The book of Proverbs was written primarily by King Solomon, considered to be the wisest man in the surrounding region; kings and queens traveled far and wide to seek his guidance. Unlike most things these days, wisdom does not have a shelf life, so Solomon's ancient words still provide some solid advice for modern-day dads. Here's what I've learned from the book: Wise men practice self-control; fools don't. Here are some other examples:

- "A quick-tempered man acts foolishly."[4]

- "An angry man stirs up strife,
  And a furious man abounds in transgression."[5]
- "A fool vents all his feelings,
  But a wise man holds them back."[6]

If you're a dad who treats home like the OK Corral, one of two things is going to happen: a showdown or a stampede. Face it, the kids will choose to fight or to run. Neither is a pretty option. When twelve-year-old Nate responded to the question, "If I could say anything to my dad, I would tell him . . . ," he wrote:

Dad, take a hike.

Most parents don't let their kids throw tantrums. Maybe the kids should put us on restriction when we throw ours. The wise man who curbs his anger uncovers his wisdom. That's simple to understand but very difficult to do. (If it were easy, we would all be wise.)

Where can you find the wisdom to exhibit self-control when your life is frustrating or you're hurting or you're afraid or injustice overcomes you? Go back to the street-smarts book, which says: "He who walks with wise men will be wise,/But the companion of fools will be destroyed."[7]

Search for a good coach and let him guide you. Find the author of the wise book and see what made him tick and what ticked him off. The wise-guy Solomon stated, "The fear of the LORD is the beginning of knowledge,/But fools despise wisdom and instruction."[8]

Behind every wise guy is a wise guy. In Solomon's case, he had a wise dad named David who led him to a wise God.

It's my prayer that I can lead my kids in the same way and leave them with the same legacy of wisdom.

Take a moment and pull out your mental address book. Who comes to mind when you ask yourself, "Who can give me the guidance I need to learn how to stop hurting my kids?" You may need to stop reading right now, bow your head, and call upon the Lord Himself. Let me remind you, from what I read in His best-seller, it is a local call, and you can get right through to the Boss!

The next step may be to take your business card off your dashboard and replace it with the number of a friend, clergyman, or counselor who can help you sort through your cart full of emotional baggage. It may be the best call you've ever made, and your kids will thank you for it.

Dads who can identify the true sources of anger, who check their weapons at the door, and who seek wisdom can heal the hurt. I've seen it happen hundreds of times. It can happen in your home too.

How would Cynda, who called her dad a "blind fool," respond if her dad walked up to her and said, "Honey, you're right. I've been a fool. I'm sorry and I'm ready to seek some wise answers for this ol' fool"? For starters, I'd bet money that Cynda (and our kids too) would be less likely to drink or take drugs. The odds for a possible crisis pregnancy would drop drastically. It's quite probable that in a year's time, almost-sixteen Cynda would sound less like hurting, seventeen-year-old Shawna, who wrote about her dad,

He has a temper,

and more like witty, seventeen-year-old Vanessa, who wrote about her khaki-clad dad,

He's very stern and solid, but he's also a dork. . . . We're exactly the same.

I don't know about you, but I'll take Vanessa's dork over Melinda's @%#$@^★.

Let's end this chapter with a message from Nicole who is fifteen. She described her dad with the color gray and wrote,

He always is grumpy or hard to get along with.

She rated her relationship with him as a two, only one notch up from the bottom. Where's the hope? It's still in Nicole's heart, for if she could say anything to her dad, she would say,

I love you [drawn with a heart] *and I wish we could have a better relationship together.*

There's hope to heal the hurting, especially when it's initiated by a wise guy called Dad.

Dear Dad,

You don't know how your actions and words really hurt me. You seem so angry, like you're burning up inside. Sometimes I want to yell. Other times I want to leave. Would you please seek some guidance and help? I still love you and I want to brighten the color of our relationship.

With love,
Your child

CHAPTER 5

Dear Dad,

Please stop
hurting you.

Love,
Your child

PLEASE STOP HURTING YOU.

*Dad, stop hurting you. The alcohol, smoking, and promiscuity aren't
going to give you what you're looking for.*
Keisha, age eighteen

My dad is full of hurt and has many scars.
Shana, age nineteen

*My dad is angry on the inside. He's got lots of hurts he's never dealt
with, but he tries to mask them on the outside.*
Anonymous survey
respondent

Seeing my dad immobilized by heart disease knocked me
off my feet. His arteries were clogged, damaging his
heart's ability to pump blood through his body. Dads are not
supposed to hurt. They are made to be invincible, right?

I learned a lot about cardiology from my father's difficult
encounter with heart attack, angina, surgery, recovery,
relapse, and recovery. Seeing my dad lying in ICU was
enough to prompt an adjustment in my own diet. When I
was growing up, my buddies always loved coming to my
house because they knew the cupboard to the left side of the
sink carried one of the finest supplies of licorice and candy
bars in town.

The Krispy Kreme doughnut shop was a local haunt for
us kids, especially with my brother working there; the shop

was owned by one of his best friend's family. I thought doughnuts were part of the four basic food groups along with hamburgers, candy, and Dr. Pepper.

At the time of my dad's heart surgery, the doctors said his heart problems were related to his triglyceride count, which measures the sugar fats, rather than his cholesterol count, which was not exceptionally high. As I watched my dad's pain I learned that a life of pies, doughnuts, and the like can maim after prolonged, extreme consumption.

Why do we hurt ourselves? As much as I have read, learned, listened, and taught, I continue to marvel at the self-destructive forces in humankind, myself included. Not only does it hurt to know someone else hurts, it grieves a child to see a parent do that to himself or herself. Dads, I've heard from our kids. They're telling us, *Please stop hurting you*.

Prior to my research, if you asked me what themes I anticipated hearing from the kids I surveyed, I would have predicted most of the messages I'm relaying to you. However, the message *Stop hurting you* would have slipped my mind. I had forgotten the pain I had felt as I watched my dad battle for his life. Somehow I had felt that my own security and health were dependent upon him; I wanted desperately to help him stop hurting.

THE INCLINATION TO CARE

Professionals working with people who have life-hurting behaviors have a word for family members who step in to help stop the hurting; we're called *caretakers*. We (I fit the role) feel the need to heal and protect. It is amazing to watch caretakers move from this kind of caring to what is called *enabling,* where they feel compelled, oftentimes because of their own need to be needed, to do everything they can to stop the other person from hurting himself or herself, even if it means the enablers hurt themselves in the process. The popular term for such a role is *codependent.* The old-fashioned word *martyr* also fits.

Kids have a natural bent to care for their parents. Their built-in, resilient love brings them back time and time again, and each time they hope their next plea will be the final request that changes their dads' behavior. This process can be illustrated by what I call "lessons from the ocean."

Along our coast, riptides are commonplace, so a system of communication has been developed that is well known by regular beachgoers. Riptides are underwater currents that pull a person away from the shore or down the shore in a parallel line with the beach. The riptide and surf swells are rated on a three-color flag system: green, yellow, and red. A green flag means calm waters. You can enter the water using normal swimming precautions, such as the rule that warns, Never turn your back to the ocean. I'm trying to relay this important message to my own children. I tell them to respect the surf and learn that a wave can be a fun acquaintance—but don't get too friendly.

The yellow flag tells swimmers and surfers to use extreme caution when entering the water due to the rip (riptide) or break (the waves). You can often spot a riptide by the brownish color of the water created by the churning sand. The size of the break, or waves, is more easily spotted from the beach, although not always. Every now and then a swell will come in and catch the happy-go-lucky bather by surprise. Let that happen once and you no longer need a lecture on respecting the ocean.

One day I went surfing despite the yellow flag. That day there was also a backwash, which occurs when the incoming waves wash up on the shore and then roll back out toward the next set of incoming waves. That can create quite a climactic moment when the two waves meet.

On this particular day, I was safe from the apex of the two crashing waves, but I did have to abandon my board during my surf ride. What caught me by surprise was my dearly beloved, pointed-nose surfboard returning to me like a faithful puppy dog. It caught the thrust of an outgoing wave and smacked me in the rear of my head. (My thick, rocklike noggin has been thumped before so you would think I would know better. At least now I come up with my head covered by my hands.) When I sat up on my board for the next humiliating pounding, I put my hand on the back of my head. When I pulled it away, blood stained my fingers.

"Hey, Todd," I called to my friend. "Would you check and see how bad my head suffered from my last extravaganza?"

After a look, Todd's diagnosis was clear: "Doug, you gotta go in. You're cut."

"Bummer." (That's how surfers talk. If I couldn't surf like one, at least I could sound like one.) I did not make a rush for shore, but I did heed my buddy's recommendation.

That evening included a mild dinner at home, a conversation with my wife, preparation for a shower, and then a calm, "Honey, would you mind taking a look at the back of my head? I kind of bumped it while surfing today."

Robin's words were few. Her body language said it all. She dropped down on the closed toilet seat as a rush of white color painted her face. "Honey, it's bad."

Seven years later, I still thank my friend Dr. J. C. Cobo for taking me into his office that night and sewing up my cranium with eleven stitches. Yellow-flag surf? Yeah, I know what it means. I've got a scar to remind me.

The final color in the three-flag warning system is red. Clearly put, a red flag means you only go in the water for one of three reasons:

1. You have no common sense (or too much testosterone).
2. You're getting paid to rescue someone else who lacks common sense.
3. You're new to the ocean and you're wondering if today is flag day.

If you're caught in the rip, you'll find yourself praying. No doubt your first supplication will be for a lifeguard to notice your inability to master the moment. Let me pass on an insight. If you're flailing with maniacal panic, no veteran lifeguard will get near you. The lifeguard is not about to jeopardize his or her own life for a swimmer who is determined to self-destruct. Lifeguards will wait for you to tire before they attempt a rescue; they know that people who are trying to hurt themselves are risky liabilities.

PULLING DAD FROM THE WATER

Kids tend to ignore life's warning-flag systems. Of course, lots of kids neglect the flags for their own actions. I call it the mythology of adolescence: the innate belief that a teenager can overcome anything if she or he so desires. I have learned some kids also avoid the same kind of guidance from veterans when it comes to rescuing their parents. After all, it's a natural instinct to want to help a parent who is hurting. Young people don't stop to think that a trained professional is better suited to rescue the victim. Instead the kids charge in, begging, "Daddy, no. Daddddyyyy, noooo!" For that matter, many adults do the same. It's difficult to sit back, watch, and wait.

Dad, I have heard it firsthand: Your child is extremely concerned about your emotional, physical, relational, and spiritual well-being. Of course, you may hear it yourself loud and clear if you are hurting them directly. Our own self-inflicted hurt, even if we see it as harmless to them, takes our children down as well. They see us hurt, and believe it or not, Dad, our self-hurting ways disconnect us from our kids.

What are dads doing to hurt themselves and hurt their relationships with their kids? The kids tell me it comes down to some primary actions: drinking, smoking, and sexual infidelity.

Alcohol Drowns a Dad's Relationship with His Child

Kids were very vocal about how alcohol drowns their relationship with their dads. One fourteen-year-old said boldly,

Dad, you need to stop drinking.

What happens between she and her dad?

He drinks a lot and doesn't pay attention to me.

In her life, Dad's drinking is a huge barrier between them. Her monologue of "I want to connect with you" is quickly disconnected.

Sixteen-year-old Brad reaches for the black felt-tip pen when coloring in his dad. Why?

He's always mad at me and drinks a lot of beer, Brad wrote.

When Brad's dad drinks, he hurts his own life and his drinking triggers his anger toward Brad. Disconnect.

Fifteen-year-old Mary can't compete with her dad's drinking:

I love you but you choose beer over your own daughter, she wrote.

Another girl named Mary also knows the pain of alcohol. She is thirteen, and she gave her dad the color black because, she said,

He was mean and he drinks. He hurt me when I was a kid. Mary is the young girl mentioned in Chapter 2, the one who said she would like to tell her dad,

You're the biggest, meanest, self-centered jerk. I hate you for what you did . . . but I love you.

Are you thinking what I'm thinking? Resilient love. Kids have it. Mary may also be like other young people who are trying so hard to perpetuate their families' secrets and myths. If asked, Mary might respond like many children of alcoholics, saying, "He doesn't really drink that much. Sssshhhh, I'm trying to keep it a secret."

Or Mary's family mythology might overshadow the presence of the hurt. It might try to create a public image that implies, *My dad is such a great guy that he really has a lot going for him.* Thus enters the myth of the father's ability to overcome his alcoholism. He's a dad, right? Isn't he invincible?

Mary has a decision to make: How will she respond to her dad and his drinking? She may have to wait for Dad's worst attempt at a red-flag day and the crisis that follows before he acknowledges his own inability to master his life.

Smoking Clouds a Dad's Relationship with His Child

Kids were also very vocal about smoking. Angel, a twelve-year-old girl, knows how destructive her dad's smoking habit is. When asked, "What would you say to your dad if you could say anything to him?" Angel answered,

Please stop smoking.

Is Angel alone? Her twelve-year-old peer Stefani had the same response to the exact same question:

Please stop smoking.

Anyone else? Yes:

eighteen-year-old Paige,

fourteen-year-old Kim,

fifteen-year-old Marrel-Ann,

thirteen-year-old Ruthie,

fourteen-year-old Gwen, and

twelve-year-old Josh, who pleads for his dad to stop smoking and drinking.

Young people are telling Dad, "Nip it in the bud!"

Whether it's drinking or smoking or sexual infidelity, your child wants you to stop hurting yourself.

Sexual Infidelity Breaks the Bond of Trust Between a Dad and His Child

Hold on to your book. Tina is a thirteen-year-old with a load of buckshot to fire:

Dad, stop being such a @#!%! and stay faithful to your wife . . . but it doesn't matter anymore, Mom is divorcing you.

Keisha's dad has mastered all three vices. She is an eighteen-year-old who gave her dad the color black because, she wrote,

He has so much hurt and pain in his heart.

What's the comment she would like to make to her dad?

Dad, stop hurting yourself. The alcohol, smoking, and promiscuity aren't going to give you what you're looking for.

Believe it or not, Keisha gave her relationship with her dad a nine on the one-to-ten scale due to an open and honest relationship. I wonder if Keisha has overcome her family secrets or myths . . .

A HARD LOOK IN THE MIRROR

Dad, are you willing to look in the mirror to see yourself as you really are? If so, join me by asking three vital questions:

- Are my actions hurting me and damaging my child in the process?
- What is driving the hurtful actions?
- Where do dads go to stop the hurt?

Are My Actions Hurting Me and Damaging My Child in the Process?

Dad, it's time for a surf report. Check the riptide and the breaking waves, because if the rip doesn't shred you, the break will pummel you. Ask yourself, "Am I doing anything to hurt myself, especially with alcohol, smoking, sex, or other areas?" Think about your life and honestly consider which warning flag applies. Be honest.

Green. I'm human and imperfect, but I consider my life to be healthy for me and my children.

Yellow. I'm yet to crash, but I'm flirting with repeating actions that will lead to an eventual crisis.

Red. Help! I need a lifeguard. I'm going down. I can't do it on my own anymore.

If you were honest, you've stepped farther than most men ever will. Now the next step is awaiting you. Are you willing to be honest with the significant people in your life?

Your child. You've probably heard the cries of his or her heart by reading some of the kids' messages in this chapter.

Your spouse. No one knows these answers better than your wife. No one.

Your friend. To what male buddy can you go and invite his input?

These are big steps, my friend. Remember, Rambo is courageous, but he's also fictional! True rescue attempts must be well supported. In the personal journey you just started, you will automatically need to answer the next question.

What Is Driving the Hurtful Actions?

The best answer to this question will not be found in this book—or in any book for that matter. Yet some valuable resources are available to help dads come in from the pounding ocean to the safety of the shore. Let me draw you back to one of the main barriers standing in the way of your relationship with your child: anger. Anger is an energy like stored-up fuel. Once it is present, it doesn't just go away because of time or denial. It's like a rushing stream of water looking for the path of least resistance. Where does anger go? Two places: out or in. First, let's talk about the anger going out.

Anger chooses the outlet of explosion. The last chapter let us know how dads are releasing the anger steam and kids are getting burned. The most obvious response of an angry person is to yell, scream, cuss, hit, attack.

Anger chooses the outlet of passive release. I used to think I was not angry because I never blew up. I've learned I have other ways to use up my mad fuel. A subtle way for me to explode is through my gift of words. (Websters and words go way back.) I mastered the art of sarcasm. Always blanketed with a smile, joke, or "I'm just kidding . . . ," my sarcastic mouth was the seep valve for my inner anger. I was angry, but I showed it with a kinder, gentler rage. Passive anger can also take the form of manipulative or sabotaging behaviors that are not easily detected by the average swimmer looking for a nice day in the ocean. Some passive angry people have perfected the ability to say, "Sure, I'd love to . . ." and as soon as the other person's back is turned, they retort, "Not likely! I'll never do that!"

Anger not only goes out toward our kids, anger goes in to hurt us dads. Here are two ways your anger may be hurting you:

Anger chooses the inlet of self-image destruction. If anger does not explode through expletives or seep through sarcasm, it will implode. Like a backwash wave that meets the shore during a high-tide swell, anger will go into your ego, especially if you never watched your role models send it out to others. Many more kids would tell you about their mad dads if they didn't take a course of self-blame. Or they are too depressed to have the strength to talk about it. Why do people do crazy stunts like going into the water on red-flag days? Sure, some kids do it for the dare or the powerful acceptance of a peer group. I have seen just as many take dangerous actions to the point of suicide attempts and successes in response to the uncontainable inner anger. Other self-hurting actions such as drug and alcohol abuse and eating disorders are often fueled by anger.

Anger chooses the inlet of bodily harm. Doctors are starting to recognize that a vast majority of health ailments are related to anger and other emotions; what was once considered scientific hogwash is now gaining respect in the practice of medicine. This new and growing field, called psychoneuroimmunology (PNI), was introduced to the consumer audience by the late Norman Cousins in his books *Head First: The Biology of Hope* and *Anatomy of an Illness*.[1]

For us laypersons, PNI is the study of how a person's emotional, spiritual, and mental states greatly influence his or her healing and well-being. In my initial years of discovering how anger affected me, I learned that my stomach was four times more likely to take an angry hit than my head was. I seldom get headaches, but every two to three months my stomach ties up in knots and makes for a miserable night's sleep. Granted there are physiological causes for this, such as a sporadic diet, limited exercise, and overwork that sometimes compound my problem by robbing me of my sleep. However, I notice that these gastro-blues don't hit me during the easygoing times. They match my own yellow-flag days. Coincidence? I doubt it.

So what can we dads do—where can we go—to stop hurting ourselves?

Where Do Dads Go to Stop the Hurt?

What do you and I do if too many yellow flags are fluttering around us? Worse yet, what if there is a red flag? Look in the mirror and ask yourself one question: "Is the hurt strong enough to convince me that I can't lead my whole life by myself?"

This is a tough question for a dad to answer honestly. After all, dads are the providers. We conquer. Dads have all the answers and the power to carry them out . . . don't we?

I can't answer the hard questions for you. It's up to you and your mirror. But let me pass along some Texas wisdom I've gleaned from Steve Arterburn, cofounder of the Minirth Meier New Life Clinics:

If someone calls you a horse, laugh.
If two people call you a horse, look in the mirror.
If three people call you a horse, saddle up!

As you consider your response to the man in your mirror, use the flag system to understand your response.

Green flag. Celebrate. You're making some good choices with your life. Consider ways you may be able to guide other men who have taken a few hits and need someone to help them better discern the ways of the water.

Yellow flag. If you can be honest about your problems, find another male with whom you can connect. You may be able to share your hurts with your wife and even with your child if you feel he or she is ready to look at what has been insidiously tormenting you—and your family. And make sure the yellow flag is appropriate for your situation. It's possible you're really encountering a red-flag problem but you hide the red flag in the lifeguard tower just to keep people happy.

Professional helpers can be invaluable on yellow-flag days. Just as lifeguards are trained to handle all kinds of life-threatening situations in the surf, professional counselors and clergy are trained to help you tackle the hurts in your life. Is there a professional in your life with whom you can meet to ask for some coaching? A no answer says more about your willingness to be taught than it does about the availability of resources.

Red flag. Red-flag days demand immediate response. Swimmers who say to themselves, "Oh, I'll be all right. The waves should die down soon," or "I'm pretty strong. I can swim through this one" are destined for disaster. They may survive . . . this time. Eventually, though, there will be consequences to face.

In the back of the book you will find a list of resources for dads who are hurting. Take the step, my friend, to stop the hurt. Your self-hurt is not just hurting you, it's disconnecting you from your child. There is hope. I've seen it happen in my life and in the lives of many, many others. Where do we dads go to find the inner healing we need? I'll let the kids offer the words of wisdom that come from the mouths of babes.

Fifteen-year-old Mickey told me of a dad who has been through a lot of stormy beaches. He doesn't live with Mickey and his mom anymore. He's now living with his folks, Mickey's grandparents. Because of the separation, Mickey only rated his relationship with his dad as a three.

Mickey, what color best describes your dad?

Brown, because he's just starting to get his act together.

Any honest, direct statement for your dad, Mickey?

I love you and want to get closer with you. Dad, keep your faith with God.

I told you there was hope. I just heard some good news for us dads who don't have our act together! We are still loved.

Nineteen-year-old Shana had suffered a great deal of pain from her dad. She said,

My dad is the color black and brown because he is full of hurt and has many scars.

How would you rate your relationship with your dad, Shana?

It's a one because he left when I was four and I never see him.

What do you want to say to your dad today?

Dad, I don't hold it against you that you left. I love you, and you don't have to be dirty. God can heal you.

I could list more than five dozen more kids who asked their dads to return to the true source of healing for hurting dads, a loving relationship with a living God. The kids became the evangelists. Now I am simply the reporter. Some kids, like Greta, have a difficult task since their dads' different religious views block their open communication. Greta said,

I want to tell you, Dad, about God but it is real hard.

Greta, you are not alone. Your peers struggle with the same thing.

Dad, this chapter has asked you and me if we can take the bad news about ourselves as expressed through the hearts of our kids. Now, can your child approach you with good news?

Earlier I introduced you to sixteen-year-old Brad. He had more comments about his relationship with his dad than with his dad's anger and drinking lots of beer:

Our relationship is a two because he doesn't understand me and why I go to church.

Any direct words to Dad, Brad?

Take the time and learn to understand me and come close to Jesus.

With his words, Brad offered his dad a solid footing to help him weather the storms in his dad's life.

Sam wrote that his dad . . .

needs to put God first in all he does and says.
Maggie, fifteen, said,
Dad, I'd love to tell you about God if you would listen.
Sabrina's words were direct and to the point:
You need Jesus, and He's the only One who can save you.

When a wise man listens closely to the heart of a child, he will become an even wiser man. With a flock of children gathered around Him, history's most noted Leader laid His hands on them and said, "Of such is the kingdom of heaven."[2]

I heard a story of a former Buddhist man who recalled a dream he once had: He found himself in the middle of raging water, fighting for his life. He cried out for help. There on shore he saw Buddha. The wise, religious man yelled swimming instructions to him. He then looked to another spot and saw Jesus. Jesus jumped into the water, swam to his side, and pulled him to safety. Then, from the security of the land, Jesus taught him how to swim.

Dad, if you're hurting and going under the pounding waves, you need a lifeguard to call on. From what I hear from kids, some dads are drowning and kids are going down with them. Hear your child's heart, for he or she is trying to save yours. Your next step may be a call for help to a friend either by phone or by prayer. There will be a hand extended to you. I know, it's pulled me out before.[3]

Dear Dad,

It hurts me to watch you hurt you. You matter too much to me to let you go down. Please call for help. I'll love you even more when you do.

Love,
Your child

CHAPTER 6

Dear Dad,

Be with me.

Love,
Your child

BE WITH ME.

*My dad and I do a lot of things together and every other Wednesday
we eat out somewhere. Our relationship is a 10!*
Karissa, age twelve

Dad, you're always busy and you don't seem to have time.
sixteen-year-old girl

My dad always takes me places.
thirteen-year-old boy

Melanie is only seven years old, but from the mouths of
babes can come the truths of life. Listen to her heart:

*I don't have a dad. Well, I do have a dad, but I don't know his
name. I only know his first name—Ron.*

What do fathers do?

*Love you. They kiss you and hug you when you need them. I
had my mom's boyfriend for a while, but they broke up.*

What would you like to do with your dad?

*I'd want him to talk to me. I wish I had somebody to talk
to. It's not fair. If two people made you, then you should still
be with those two people. I'm not so special. . . . I don't have
two people.*

What would Daddy be like?

*It would be like the commercial where the kids say, "Daddy, are
you all right?" The kids show the daddy that they care for him.
They put a thermometer in his mouth. They think he's sick because*

*he came home early. They are sitting on the couch watching TV,
and it's like, "Wow, we can play with Dad!"*

*One day when I get older, I'm gonna go back to Georgia (to the
Army) and try to find my dad.*

At only age seven Melanie has offered one of the most
insightful presentations on family values I have seen in a long
time. She talks about the power of personal touch, the
importance of intimacy, the need for two-parent families,
and the value of dads.

Listen up, Dad. Our kids have the wisdom to help you
and me succeed in fatherhood.

Here is a final message of the first cry of the heart, the cry
to *connect*. The message from your child is, *Dad, be with me.*
A child's desire to be with his or her father is the breeding
ground for their relationship. The *Be with me* message caps
the five messages defining a child's need to connect:

> *I love you.*
> *Please accept me.*
> *Please don't hurt me.*
> *Please stop hurting you.*
> *Be with me.*

This fifth and final message of the monologue is the last
one-way statement from the child to the father. Dads don't
need to respond verbally to meet the need behind this
message. We have to act. Kids don't want our advice; they
want our presence.

Kristin, a fourteen-year-old, says:

Dad, I love you and I love when you spend time with me.

Joy, now a grown woman of twenty-six, lends some encouragement to us dads who think of the day when our own kids will reach adulthood. She rated her relationship with her dad as a ten because, she wrote,

We connect.

Joy has what every kid is crying for: to connect with dad, not merely to coexist.

Seventeen-year-old Ryan is grateful for the time spent with his dad. He ranked his relationship with his dad as an eight because, he said,

We do a lot together.

Ryan, what would you tell your dad if you could say anything?

Dad, I wish I could have known you when you were my age.

Sounds like one friend talking to another. Ryan's dad must be quite a guy. Obviously, he's heard and responded to Ryan's message, *Be with me.*

What was a highlight for fifteen-year-old Ellie?

We went to a father-daughter dance.

That helped earn a nine rating on the scale!

One young man described his dad as the color gray because,

I don't know my dad; we moved from Japan to the U.S. when I was eight. I've seen him twice since then.

Children will never know their dads unless the dads first have the time to be with their kids. What would this young man tell his dad the next time he sees him if he could say anything?

Dad, I wish I was a more important part of your life.

Do you hear the meaning behind the message? Our kids

equate time spent with you and me as our estimate of their value. Kids think, "I am important to my dad because he wants to be with me. I matter to him!"

Dad, we matter, and child after child after child has told me so. You and I not only have a very influential role, we also are in pursuit of a very difficult task. If your life is anything like mine, it is not easy to be a father. One of my favorite writers offered some empathy when he arrived at the same conclusion. Tim Hansel wrote in *What Kids Need Most in a Dad:* "There aren't enough honest books for dads that admit to the intense strain and adventure of being a father."[1]

Dad, you're not alone. I'm right there with you. And so is Tim Hansel and millions of other dads. What makes it such a challenge? I've done some thinking about how to respond to our children's *Be with me* message, and I want to pass on my thesis on "The Economics of Fatherhood."

THE ECONOMICS OF FATHERHOOD

We fathers are caught between the economics of time and the economics of supply and demand as we try to answer our kids' cry to *Be with me.*

The Economics of Time

Fathering is like cramming a size-ten foot in a size-seven shoe. I have decided I don't have enough time to meet all my obligations since I figure I would need twenty-eight hours in a day. I want to help with the family life, so I'll pitch in periodically for the car pool. Then it's off to work, where I'm striving to lead a not-for-profit organization to make a difference in the lives of young people and families. Then there is the challenge of managing people in the workplace. I'm still a novice, so the task of guiding and supporting fellow workers often takes more of a toll than I like to let on. I try to serve with care, integrity, and a commitment to conflict resolution—great stuff, which takes more time than the "just go do your job until I tell you otherwise" approach. The day seems to gallop by, and before I know it, it's over.

Hope against hope that you don't get a call like I just did from my wife as I sit here writing this chapter, "Honey, hi . . . uh, well . . . the van won't start."

Of course. We just placed an ad to sell our van and buy a newer one before the upcoming, annual "let's pack five bodies in a vehicle for a ten-hour trip to the grandparents' house" vacation.

Come five-ish, I'll look up from the computer, the phone, or meetings with people and realize the day is spent.

By this time my family has moved into what we call the pit hours: 4 to 7 P.M. FST (family standard time). The cosmic forces of fatigue and hunger collide in a small setting called the kitchen, and I come riding in on my white horse with the hope of bringing relief. (Ideally arriving at least within twenty minutes of the actual time I told my wife I would be home.) Like a team wrestler, my wife, Robin, tags my hand and says, "You go get 'em."

Why is it that all telemarketers of the nation descend upon our house during the pit hours? We survive yet another dinner meal of intimacy and personal exchange (*right . . . just get through it without a battle, and we're happy*). Then I move into the drill-sergeant mode by barking commands to all corners of the house regarding homework, clothes, brushed teeth, going to the bathroom, finding the missing "favorite, can't sleep without them" pajamas, remembering the cupcakes that need to be baked for tomorrow's class party, and the list goes on . . .

By the time I land in a reclined position, it's 9 P.M. I realize I am a little sluggish because I have not worked out in a week. Exercise? Love to. When is the next chance I can get into the weight room for a good workout? How about after my last child's high school graduation ceremony? My heart breaks for single parents. I don't know how they survive.

I have not even begun to talk about time with friends, extended family, volunteering to make my community a better place to live, and working with the kids at church. And what about yard work? Car maintenance? Who can afford to pay a guy forty-five dollars per hour to change the car's air filter? And then there's the latest novel I've been wanting to read . . . Forget it! I'm happy to get a 110-minute movie escape every few months . . . and I'm talking about renting the movie. Sometimes I start to think I haven't been in a theater since Reagan was president.

Dad, is your life any different? Probably not. Now add your kid's message, *Be with me.*

A fifteen-year-old girl described her dad as the color plaid because,

He's always busy and doesn't seem to have time.

Ouch!

Do you ever feel like your life is one big checklist of

expectations running together? Time is a priceless commodity in limited supply for today's dads.

The Economics of Supply and Demand

What are the "discouraging forces" putting the brakes on Dad's ability to respond to his child's *Be with me* message? I call them "The Six Adversaries of Fatherhood":

1. Financial demands. Raising kids is expensive. Families need roofs over their heads. (And, of course, we have to pay for the repair bill when the roof leaks!) The American dream of owning a home is a huge commitment; don't let anyone tell you otherwise. Gone are the days of bachelorhood when a sleeping bag, a lukewarm shower, and a cold pizza equaled domesticity. Unless you are independently wealthy, most dads are struggling to make ends meet. Buried in the financial pull are a few other not-so-obvious monetary demands:

Materialistic kids. Let's be honest, our kids are inundated with the marketing ploys of the advertising world. The kiddie market has reached seventy-five billion dollars, 2 percent of the economy.[2] Where is the fun money going? Over ten billion is spent on such games. Or just try driving past McDonald's or Burger King en route to Larry's Discount Burger and watch Junior go ballistic in the backseat of the minivan. These franchise moguls know how to market to our kids. And we no longer own just one American dream home. Your daughter can spend up to four hundred dollars on a Barbie mansion. Where do our kids get the money? Dad, of course. And what if Dad can't supply it all? Now enters money demand number two:

Working mothers. If your family is fortunate enough to have two parents living under the same roof, it is likely that both are working to buy the house and raise the kids.

Don't forget about taking care of Mom's needs. I was reading an article in *Men's Health* about the challenges facing today's dads. It was entitled, "Where's Papa?"[3] How fitting. No sooner do I turn the page and there, staring me in the face, is an advertisement for diamonds from $950 . . . just because you love her. Don't worry, they've provided a toll-free number for your convenience. Where's Papa? He's working off the diamond bracelet he just gave Mom. Don't get me wrong; a diamond is forever. It's just that the credit card payment seems nearly that long too.

The more we crank up the demand on our finances, the more pressure we feel to supply and the more time it takes away from our families to deliver the goods. Dad, how much of your family's financial lifestyle is mortgaging your ability to provide what your child is really looking for—your time? How would your family respond if you decided to reduce the cash flow by 10 percent to free up a chunk of your time to be at home? Do they want you or your checkbook? Unless the family decides, you and I will never be able to do both and live to tell the story.

2. More roles for dads. Let's face it—our dads were not reading books like this one forty years ago. I truly believe there are more demands placed on today's dad to be an active, interpersonal, dynamic force in the life of his child. Maybe I'm perpetuating it right now. The title character in the movie *Mr. Mom* would have been as alien as a creature from outer space to a 1950s audience. Dads of previous generations did have demands, some even more difficult in the work and economic environment. But today's dad role is more demanding than Ozzie Nelson's role in the 1950s. Today we have to be good ol' Dad, Mr. Mom, and the New Father.

3. More threatening cultural demands. Our kids today are growing up in a world unknown to you and me. As we say around NIYM, "We were ten, twelve, sixteen once, but we were never their age. They face so much at such a young age." The treacherous cliffs we played near are still there, but today the guardrails—the boundaries and authorities to guide young people—are absent.

I remember as a fourteen-year-old going to Disneyland for an eighth-grade graduation party. A buddy and I were acting like big shots while driving the cars in Autopia. When we turned a corner, we switched cars, thinking we were in the cover of the overpass. No sooner had we sped off than two Disneyland employees came out of the bushes. We got the lecture of our lives and almost spent the rest of the day sitting in the chartered bus waiting for our classmates to return.

Mischievous behavior is surely not a late-twentieth-century phenomenon. What's lacking today is the presence of adult authorities reprimanding young people for wrong behavior. Today, no one's watching our kids. They are driving dangerously close to the cliff, and the world lacks human or moral guardrails to keep them on track. Dad, it's a tough job today to steer our kids through life.

Bottom line: Dad, you will need to spend more resources

battling the negative aspects of today's culture than any parents in previous generations. A study among junior-high students found the prime determinant of drinking or drug use is how many hours the child is left alone during the week.[4]

No longer will kids simply crash the borrowed car to do something risky or to let off their anger. Today, with drugs, alcohol, suicide, violence, crisis pregnancy, we're playing for keeps. And family crisis is expensive. It costs twenty-one thousand dollars each year per child at Boys Town. That's nothing compared with the forty-five thousand dollars it costs each year to raise a child at Children's Village in New York.[5] Yet all those costs are still nothing compared to the loss of our children's potential.

To face and fight today's culture, our kids need us more than ever. Dad, we no longer prepare our children *for* the world; we ready them *against* the world.

4. Limited role models. As we look for guidance in this challenging role, we are hard-pressed to find effective fathers to model. If I wanted to excel in a sport, I would find a pro in that sport's field and learn everything I could from him. Why do you think sports-training videos are such smash hits? Weekender guys like you and me are buying them to try to drop a few more strokes off the game. But where do we go to find the pro dad in our world?

5. Painful broken past. Some dads are facing an uphill battle due to the war wounds from their relationships with their own fathers. If your dad did not hear your message of *Be* *with me,* you missed two things: confirmation of your value and examples of what a dad does with his child. You are on your own to establish a new father–child relationship. Your pain or ignorance may keep you away from your child more than you know or care to acknowledge.[6]

6. *Hurting marriages.* A painful marriage, whether present or past, will undermine virtually every effort of a caring dad. Given the choice between a stronger marriage and a more active role as a parent, invest in your marriage. It will trickle down on the kids; water never flows uphill. Good parenting doesn't foster good marriages, but good marriages do make for healthy kids. Divorce can make Dad's job real tough, no matter how much he may want to be with his children. For the parent who does not have full-time custody, the spontaneous and ongoing opportunities to interact with a child are lost. Yet many of life's wonderful moments are not staged, booked, and forced; they happen off the cuff—around the dinner table, on the way to school in the car, while working in the yard together over the weekend.

For fourteen-year-old Matt and his dad, the car is their private meeting place. He said,

I always talk to my dad about stuff in the car.

It is difficult for a visiting dad to say, "OK, son, let's create a significant moment together during my visit with you this evening to meet your need of being with me."

I've just listed six adversaries of fatherhood that drag us down in our efforts to lift up our kids. What do we do to overcome these adversaries? Let's turn again to the wisdom of those we are trying to serve—our kids. Here are four questions to ask your child and yourself to better meet his or her message of *Be with me.*

FOUR QUESTIONS FOR YOU AND YOUR CHILD

1. Do My Kids Really Want to Spend Time with Me?

The kids in my survey said yes. But I can't answer for your child. Does your child want your time? If your children are too young to respond to that question, just assume they do. You'll be right. If they do catch your drift and they deny the need, don't give up. Listen very closely to their hearts, not just to their words. Walking right up to your teenage son and saying, "Son, do you want to spend time with me?" may trigger a host of surprised responses. He may think, *Not right now,* or, *Not if you're looking for something,* or, *Not if I did something wrong,* or, *Not if you're going to keep acting this weird.*

I suggest you try an experiment. Invest the time without asking the question again and watch what happens. (I'm going to suggest some practical ideas to help us dads connect with our kids later in the chapter.)

2. Do I Believe They Want to Spend Time with Me?

Do we dads really believe our kids want time with us, need time with us, and benefit from time with us? You are hearing it from me as someone who is behind the front lines with kids. Believe me, they want time with us. Listen to the heart of your child and you'll hear a small voice from a young person's soul saying, *Dad, I want to connect with you, so please be with me.*

Thirteen percent of one survey group (174 kids) wanted to tell their dads how important their dads' time is to them. Let me drop some names:

Robert, age fifteen: *My dad spends a lot of time with me, but I wish he were home a little more.*

Shannon, age fifteen: *My dad's and my relationship is a two because he is too busy for me and never talks to me or spends time with me.*

Margaret, age sixteen: *My dad is the color blue cuz I picture him in the clouds a lot of the times. He's too busy to do things with me. Our relationship is only a six because of it.*

Stacy, a sixteen-year-old male: *My dad and I are at a ten because he spends so much time with me.*

Jonathan, a fourteen-year-old, caps the words in his response: *THANKS FOR SPENDING TIME WITH ME!*

In a grouping of twenty-seven young people who used the phrase "spend time" when writing about their dads, thirteen echoed Jonathan's thanks, eleven were sad for the time not spent, and three requested more time.

How did these kids rate their dads? Here are the average ratings for each group:

Grateful kids 8.83
Sad kids 6.0
Hoping kids 7.33

Which kids rated their dads a ten? You're right, the grateful kids; five out of the thirteen kids said their relationship with Dad was a ten!

Are you convinced yet? Time is a valuable commodity to a child who has no other real tangible good or asset. If you're still doubting the priority of the message *Be with me,* I could easily turn to a few others like Meredith, Summer, Kelly, Paul, Mark, Ruthanne, Tim, Brandy, Frank, Joanna, Jessica, Cameron . . . They all said they want time with Dad.

Now, a question for us dads.

3. Do I Want to Spend More Time with My Child?

Don't answer this one too quickly. It would be easy to say, "Of course! Don't most dads?" Well, yes, most dads do—most of the time. But let me offer another perspective: Dads don't *always* want to spend time with their kids. I know it's risky to stand up in today's "family-values" environment and say, "I don't get much personal benefit from being with my kids" or "I find greater satisfaction and less conflict by investing my time and energy into my work. It gives me the rush I want, and I need to feel like I am a man who is worth something. I'm slaying dragons, building empires, closing deals, conquering new lands. Frankly, playing Nintendo with an eight-year-old to get my initials up on the TV screen does not do anything for me."

Playing the role of dad does not always give a man the "thrill of victory" or the "challenge of the battle." I came across a survey of young men who, on the surface, wanted what many other males want. The top priorities in the lives of these eighteen- to twenty-four-year-old men were:

1. A successful career (32 percent)
2. A happy marriage (30 percent)
3. To contribute to society (16 percent)
4. Well-adjusted children (9 percent)[7]

Check the numbers. Only 9 percent, not even one in ten, hold well-adjusted children as a top priority in their lives! Are they ogres? Probably not. Although it is likely most of them are not parents yet. A man's opinions may change as the presence of a little diaper-wrapped blessing arrives in his life. He may care a whole lot less about a successful career or contributing to society. But there may still be a hidden proviso. He may subconsciously determine *I will not be involved beyond the point that my participation will reduce my success or earnings.*

Dad, the core question is: How do you personally define success? If you don't place a great deal of value in fathering your child, investing time will be a very costly expense. Your child will know your heart is not in the effort. Children just know.

4. How Can I Spend More Time with My Child?

I'm going to suggest three action steps to accomplish this goal:

Action step 1: Involve your child in the family demands, especially financial ones. Most kids don't know what it costs to raise a family. They think we want to go to work. (And they probably fear we are not thinking of them while we are working.) Dad, help your child understand and at the same time lower the financial demands that take you away from him or her. Does the family really need a new car? Would driving rather than flying on your vacation provide the same value to your family?[8] You will not only lessen the demand on you, you will raise more responsible children in the process.

Fifteen-year-old Kevin definitely needed to see the demands he was placing on his dad. He rated his relationship with Dad this way:

It's a five because he is at work most of the time so we don't do things.

Kevin, what would you like to pass on to your dad if you could say anything?

Can I have some money?

Kevin, let me shoot straight with you. The economics of supply and demand says you can't have both. It's hard for Dad to provide Nintendo, $150 basketball shoes, a car next year when you turn sixteen . . . with insurance . . . and spend more time with you and less time at work. Two equal and opposite forces cannot coexist without pulling one apart. If you want more time with Dad, something's gotta give.

Dad, the Kevins of the world need to see the bigger picture. Let your kids help you choose your priorities. They may forgo the new shoes for a cheaper pair if it means being able to play one-on-one with Dad. (It's interesting to note that only six out of fifteen hundred responses to my survey stated they wanted more money from Dad, including Kevin's.)

Like many dads in my community, Bill's dad commutes to work. At sixteen, Bill sees this travel as a competitor. He rated his relationship with his dad as an eight, but said,

My dad works so far away we can't talk as much as I would like.

Bill's words directed to his dad were,

Dad, I love you and I want you to come home and spend more time.

Sixteen-year-old Erica understands her dad's dilemma. She says to him,

I love you, and I am glad that you work hard to make money for the family although you aren't home.

Action step 2: Involve them in your work world. For some young people, *work* is a four-letter word, an evil power taking Dad away from his family. Fourteen-year-old Kelli said,

Our relationship could be higher (than an eight) *if he didn't have to work so hard.*

Work is the mistress seducing dads' time, energy, and emotion. If we come home from the workplace drained and despondent, our kids begin to hate this thing because it hurts us. Seventeen-year-old Jess said her dad comes home

grumpy from work.

Seventeen-year-old Becca said,

Purple is the color for my dad because he has to work instead of coming to my games.

More than four dozen kids out of all fifteen hundred wanted to tell me about the role of work in their dads' lives. How many would you guess spoke positively about Dad's hard work, seeing it as part of his commitment to his family? 50 percent? 30 percent? 25 percent?

Only 16 percent, or one in six kids who mentioned Dad's work, considered it a positive force in the family. That means five out of every six young people consider work to be a rival in their relationship with their dads.

How do we help our families understand our work world? Invite them to come along and see for themselves. My dad was an electrical engineer. I told my friends he drove trains. What did I know about his working on radar systems for a major defense contractor? I never saw the inside of my dad's work world.

If you can't take your children with you, call them during the day while you are working. If you have a cellular phone, call them while you're driving; they're worth the cost of the call. It may be hard for you to understand why this is important to your kids. After all, you and I seldom want another phone call to answer, but your child lives for it. By taking the time to make that call your child gets the message, *Wow, Dad was thinking of me while he was at work today. I must be more important than his work stuff.*

If your children are still little, play work at home. Teach them what you do, and let them be the workers. And whenever you can, include them in the work you do around the house. One young man named Joe said his relationship with his dad was a nine. They work and play together. Alexis said,

Dad, don't spend so much time working and spend more time with us.

Kensie echoed Alexis's comments. Could Kensie go to

work with her dad a time or two and better understand him? When Dad is drawn away by the big, bad work-wolf, Kensie would then know what he is doing. She could visualize his day and appreciate what he does to serve his family's financial needs.

A lot of dads would love to choose the Daddy Track over the Fast Track. In a survey a few years ago conducted by the polling firm Yankelovich Clancy Shulman, 48 percent of the men who responded said they would stay home if given the choice; 51 percent said they would work.[9]

How about you? Does your child know how much you would enjoy staying home and playing all day with him or her? Do your weekend activities—golf or watching football—say otherwise?

I talked to one young woman named Sharon who said her dad literally never had time for her. She often approached him, but he would respond, "Not now Sharon; I don't have the time."

"Then," Sharon told me, "I would watch him move into the family room, turn on the TV, and disappear for hours." She started to cry as she talked to me about her dad.

I asked, "Could you ever write him a letter to share some of your feelings?"

"I mentioned that one day to my mom," she said. "But she guaranteed me my dad would never read it."

How will the Sharons of the next generation know how to love their kids?

You may be wondering, "Can I have both? Can I be a company vice president working sixty hours a week and retain a flex schedule to make it to my son's soccer game?"

It all comes down to your definition of success. Allow me to reference the excellence experts, Thomas Peters and Nancy Austin in *A Passion for Excellence.*

> We have found that the majority of passionate activists who hammer away at the old boundaries have given up family vacation, Little League games, birthday dinners, evenings, weekends, and lunch hours. . . . We are frequently asked if it is possible to "have it all"—a full and satisfying personal life and a full and satisfying hardworking professional one. Our answer is: no. The price of excellence is time, energy, attention, and focus.[10]

Dad, it is highly unlikely for anyone to have both. Some do it, but most can't. Kids are not easily contained in a Day-Timer.

Action step 3: Moving beyond guilt to influence. My wife and I went on a date three years ago. No, that is not the last time we dated, but sometimes it feels like it. I highly recommend dating your wife. It may be the best action step you could ever take for your role as a dad.

We were sitting in front of a yogurt shop, discussing what we call "high summits" (the latest family-agenda items). That night it was my night to lead the conversation. I told her, "Honey, I have three things I would like to talk about: First, money. Second, sex. And third, children."

I know what you are thinking—"not enough of the first two and too much of the third." You're close, but I won't bore you with the details of the first two topics. I'll jump right to the third: children. I said, "Hon, I feel like it's time for us to have a third child."

"Really?" she responded. (She did not gasp or faint or exclaim, "Wow!")

"Yes. Our family is working. We're far from perfect, but I feel like we need to be stewards of the love the four of us have by sharing it with another person." (I paused to accentuate my suggestion.)

"Plus, I'd love to try for a boy." (OK, my testosterone got in the way.)

For a few months I had been evaluating my life and journaling the thoughts that were coming to my mind. I found myself asking, "Where is my life best invested?" I was facing some professional changes and opportunities. In the middle of this season of introspection, I came across a quote by Dag Hammarskjöld, former secretary-general of the United Nations, that grabbed my heart: "It is more noble to give yourself completely to one individual than to labor diligently for the salvation of the masses."[11]

Dad, I don't know about your life's passion, but I'm striving to "live life on purpose." I'm only here once, and I want to make the most of it. That's why this man's wisdom rocked my soul. The more effective approach is to love the individual down the hall, not to reach the masses around the world.

Since then, guilt has not been my motivator, for it is a short-term prompter. I am a papa for the power of the position. I have learned that power lies not in the ability to persuade distant adults to buy into your dream, but in the responsibility (response-ability) to serve your children in realizing their dreams.

Dad, when you hear the *Be with me* message, move

beyond guilt. Let the guilt of your preoccupied past prompt you to pursue forgiveness from your child, remembering that your kid has childlike, resilient love. Then move on, and find the incredible joy of helping another person succeed.

Somewhere in Atlanta there is a dad who knows what I mean. I'll let his son speak on his behalf:

> Growing up in Atlanta, I can't remember not having a basketball or baseball in my hand when school was out. I was always doing something athletic and my father always supported that. He was supportive, but not pushy. My father and mother went to every game I played, but my dad wouldn't embarrass himself or me by acting like some of the other fathers. And while some of the other guys have long since given up baseball, what my father did was make me want to improve and continue to play.[12]
>
> —Wally Joiner, Kansas City Royals
> pro baseball player

I am not asking you to live out your dreams vicariously through your children. Story after story is told of a dad who is striving to make his son become something the dad never was. I am talking of vivacious (not vicarious) life-giving. Dad, you are a giver of life. Your relationship with your child's mother germinated his or her life. You took the lead. Don't let this influence stop at conception.

Moving beyond guilt means maximizing the mini times. Paul Lewis, a parenting-world colleague, suggests we dads consider "five-minute fathering possibilities."[13] He urges dads to look for small moments of fathering opportunities, like wrestling with the kids when we first get home.

My two older kids know a quick predinner run to the corner convenience store for a treat only takes a few minutes and fifty-nine cents per child. (Kind of a funny outing for a dad who abstains from the sugar stuff for health reasons. My life is a paradox.) You may also be amazed to find how quickly you can get the bikes out of the garage and take one quick lap around the neighborhood. It builds up the kids, strengthens your role as the dad, buys Mom some time, and bypasses the heat of the pit hours. It makes for a win-win-win situation. Paul Lewis suggests writing a list of these five-minute fathering ideas in your datebook and adding to it whenever new ideas come to mind.

Living beyond guilt may mean jumping the corporate ship. Some dads take what seems like the ultimate step in moving beyond guilt to influence their children: They jump the corporate ship. Before his son, Jesse, was born, Dan Russell was tour manager for the rock group U2, on the road with the band ten out of twelve months a year. He gave it up to spend more time with his son. And the result: "Fifty percent less money is worth 100 percent more happiness. Somebody else can do this job," he said in an interview.[14]

Peter Lynch hung up his thirteen-billion-dollar mutual fund to do good deeds and have more time with his family. Other guys have made a similar priority shift but not without paying a price. Houston Oilers offensive tackle David Williams missed a 1993 football game against the New England Patriots because he chose to be with his wife as she gave birth to their first child, a son. Williams's bosses docked him $111,111, a week's pay. The team insisted that Williams could have flown into Boston the night of the birth and arrived in time for the game the next day. Williams said he couldn't find a flight, but he really did not try too hard. He wanted to be with his son. The Oilers won the game, an unusual occurrence in the 1993 season.[15]

These examples illustrate how three prominent dads took steps to honor their children's spoken or unspoken message, *Be with me*. They broke new ground in a world where Dad's first role is assumed to be his work. Granted, at least two of these guys, maybe all three, had a nice financial lifeboat to land in when they jumped ship. Some of us guys don't have quite the income margin to step out of the game and be thrown for a financial loss. (In many ways, it's guys like us trusting guys like Peter Lynch that afforded him the chance to choose the Daddy Track. Of course, investments in the hands of wizards like Peter are a valuable way for ordinary dads to sock some money away today to lessen tomorrow's financial demands, thereby giving us more time to play with our kids.)

Living beyond guilt means investing the time. When Charlie Shedd, a former syndicated columnist and family advocate, now retired, asked hundreds of young people the attributes of "One Neat Dad" he came up with the most-appreciated qualities.

1. He takes time for me.
2. He listens to me.
3. He plays with me.
4. He invites me to go places with him.

5. He lets me help him.
6. He treats my mother well.
7. He lets me say what I think.
8. He's nice to my friends.
9. He only punishes me when I deserve it.
10. He isn't afraid to admit when he's wrong.

Shedd wrote, "Note: Qualities one to five are versions of the single word, *Time!*"[16]

Dad, why not ask your child to provide twenty responses to the following statement, "I love to . . ." If you're willing, make up your own list ahead of time and see how closely your lists correspond. Once you have your child's list, take each item as an activity for you and your child to do together. You may find yourself watching a sunset, playing Frisbee in the park, running through sprinklers, eating ice cream at the mall, watching Saturday-morning cartoons in your pajamas, playing Marco Polo in the pool, riding a whirlpool in a Jacuzzi, making mud pies in the sandbox, praying for a neighbor's pets, singing movie songs in the car, hacking on the computer, cruising the mall for the ultimate sale, taking swings in a batting cage . . . the list can go on and on. It's not what you do that matters; it is simply, *You matter.* And spending your time with your child lets your child know he or she matters to you.

I heard a story of a successful attorney who said,

The greatest gift I ever received was a gift I got one Christmas when my dad gave me a small box. Inside was a note saying, "Son, this year I will give you 365 hours—an hour every day after dinner. It's yours. We'll talk about what you want to talk about, we'll go where you want to go, play what you want to play. It will be your hour!" My dad not only kept his promise, but every year he renewed it, and it's the greatest gift I ever had in my life. Today, I am the result of his time.[17]

Remember Melanie, our fatherless, seven-year-old family-values expert mentioned in the beginning of this chapter? Did you catch her comment about her imaginary dad coming home and the kids playing nurse? They think he's sick because he came home early!

Your child may not get it when you make the shift. Your wife may not understand. Don't be alarmed if they reach for the thermometer. But you and I will know otherwise . . . it'll be our secret.

The message *Be with me* provides the transition from *connect,* the first phase in the growth of the father-child relationship, to the next: *relate.* A dad who hears this message and is present battles the absence barrier that often infects the end of the first stage, monologue, and then contaminates the second stage of a child's growth, the dialogue. Unless you have responded to the five messages of your child's cry to connect—

I love you,
Accept me,
Please don't hurt me,
Please stop hurting you,
Be with me—

you cannot move to this next level.

When a child comes from a family striving to connect during the preschool and early-elementary-school years, he or she will make a natural move into the second era, the years of the "dialogue stage" during the preteen to midteen years.

I've found that the first phase—connecting—is a critical foundation to the second—relating. Lost time is costly (it may take more effort to break through barriers of past behaviors and negative consequences), but teenagers and even adult children can reconnect with their dads. Then they are ready to begin the intimate relationship of the second phase of dialogue. Now the child needs a response from you. If you have established a base of connectedness in the first phase, you can go on to hear and respond to your child's next three messages:

Listen to me,
Forgive me, and
Be real with me.

Dear Dad,

Please be with me. Just spending time with you makes me feel so important, like I really matter to you.

Love,
Your child

PART
THREE

THE KIDS' DIALOGUE:

I want to relate to you.

WHAT KIDS SAY . . .

I want you to listen to me.
Summer, age sixteen

My dad respects my opinions.
Samuel, age fifteen

Dad, you're the best dad in the world because you help me with my problems.
Justus, age seventeen

My dad is kind of secret. I don't know him really.
Wendy, age sixteen

WHAT KIDS MEAN . . .

Listen to me,

Forgive me, and

Be real with me.

WHAT KIDS NEED . . .

A dad who listens to the words and hears the heart of his child.

A dad who forgives once and for all.

A dad who takes off his mask and becomes real.

CHAPTER 7

Dear Dad,

Listen to me.

Love,
Your child

LISTEN TO ME.

I want you to listen to me the way you like me to listen to you.
Meredith, age sixteen

My dad respects my opinions and he will always listen to me when others don't.
Samuel, age fifteen

My dad and I argue and fight a lot. We are not really good at listening to each other.
Kari, age thirteen

Dad, are you listening? The message is loud and clear. Listen. I admit, few dads are going to read this chapter and be surprised by their kids' strong desire to be listened to. Even fewer guys will disagree with my next observation: Dads are the last ones to know. One perplexed father said, "I've got TV, cable, two phone lines, a phone in my car, and a fax, and my kids tell me I'm out of touch!"

Why? Dad, we can blame it on our schedules. We can attribute it to "nobody ever lets me know." Yet the truth may be as simple as this: We were not listening. Ask our wives.

Do you remember when your child used to ramble incessantly? Words were plentiful, and meaning was insignificant. We dads could offer an occasional, "Uh-huh . . ." and like an Indy race-car driver coming in for a pit stop, that verbal acknowledgment was enough to refuel the youngster and send him or her out for more laps.

My daughter, Brookelyn, is like an engine running out of gas that winds up to higher RPMs before it stalls. The more tired she becomes, the faster she talks about meaningless things with little expectation of response from my wife or myself. Before we know it, especially on long, late-night drives home from somewhere, she is fast asleep.

Somewhere in the preteen years, around ten to eleven for boys and nine to ten for girls, a shift takes place. A kid's relationship moves from the monologue to the dialogue stage. I know my daughter will change in the next few years. One day we'll be driving home, and in the middle of her dissertation, she'll say, "Dad, you're not listening." Thus will commence the era of the dialogue.

The message *Listen to me* was not placed in the dialogue phase by accident. Now that your child has reached a stage when he or she is ready to talk, the youngster wants someone there to listen, preferably you. The child's heart is crying out to relate.

Until one human being truly hears and understands the core of another person's meaning, communication remains a game called "let's pretend." One young person stated the game quite clearly:

My dad and I both always have to get our points across, so we disagree about everything and spend our lives trying to get our points across.

Like lobbing verbal hand grenades into the enemy's foxhole, the dad and his child are hoping somebody will hit a target.

Dad, connecting (the first phase of the dad-child relationship) is the prerequisite for a healthy relationship (phase two) between father and child. Here are some ways you can develop a healthy relationship.

LISTEN UP!

I ran the numbers again. They repeat the pattern we've seen before. The dad who hears the particular message of the child ranks high on the one-to-ten scale. The dad who doesn't hear it doesn't rate well.

Out of all fifteen hundred surveys, the average ratings (on the one-to-ten scale) given to dads by kids who used the word *listen* in their descriptions of them were:

Dads who listen well: 9.27
Dads who don't listen: 4.30
Dads whose kids ask them to listen more: 8.00

Dad, listen up. The 9.27 average rating is one of the highest I've seen for dads with any one particular quality or characteristic. More than half of the people who said their dads listened well rated their father a ten and referred to his listening as a key to his success. Sounds like listening rings a bell with kids. The bulk of the survey participants from whom I have gleaned input are in their teenage years. At this age, young people are just beginning to feel that they have something to say, and they desperately want someone to listen.

REPLACE THE REFRIGERATOR

Ron James, CEO of the Minnesota operations of US West Communications and cochairman of the state's

Action for Children Commission, grew up in a poor black family headed by a single mother. He knows firsthand the consequences of a missing father. As an advocate for kids and a telecommunications expert, he's got a powerful insight for today's dads: "The new mode of communication between parents and children is through notes held to refrigerators by magnets."[1]

Stop reading for a moment and take a walk to the fridge in your home. Is it like my house? The hub of communications around which the entire family revolves? You're not alone. Welcome to the family E-mail. How did families survive before the refrigerator? Did they tape notes to the icebox? Or the hearth above the fireplace?

Dad, it's time to replace the refrigerator. You can do it. You're big enough and man enough to fend off the prowess and agility of a major kitchen appliance. Just don't stand in the way if your child is looking for food, especially a teenage boy. Talk to him after he eats.

Now that we know who is the boss in the family and who is left out in the cold, I'm ready to pass on some keen insights from the experts: the kids.

THE KIDS' LISTENING TIPS

1. Listen Within Earshot

Togetherness is the breeding ground for true communication. Unless Dad and his child are together, they'll never talk. I know it seems obvious, but until you and I remove the second A-barrier between us and our kids—absence—we will never relate to them.

One young person told me,

My relationship with my dad is a ten. Why? My dad listens to me when I want to talk to someone.

What else?

My dad takes me places. . . . Dad, if I could tell you anything, I want you to know I love you. . . . The color blue best describes my dad because he is calm and doesn't yell much.

Listen to this kid's comments about his dad, who is meeting four of his child's needs:

1. My dad listens. *(Listen to me.)*
2. My dad takes me places. *(Be with me.)*
3. Dad, I love you. *(I love you.)*
4. He is calm and doesn't yell much. *(Stop hurting me.)*

No A-barriers blocking this father-child relationship. Who is this guy? The Clark Kent of dads? A Barry Bonds–type long-ball hitter? (There goes the curve, guys. He just bumped it up another notch.)

To listen to our kids, we dads have to be close enough often enough to hear them.

2. Listen Without Judging

What picture does the word *lecture* conjure up in your mind? A dull monologue by a boring professor? Your child probably would envision an adult rambling in a nonstop fashion about highly irrelevant ideas for the purpose of boasting his own abilities at the cost of the listener's interest, participation, and possibly, self-esteem.

Dad, do you listen to hear, or do you listen to gather fuel for your next lecture?

Eighteen-year-old Don told me,

My dad is like the color gray. He tries to remain neutral and passive when listening to my argument and beliefs.

Dad, do you give your child the room Don has to disagree? In Melissa's house, it's not all right to think differently from Dad. Her relationship with her dad ranks a four because, she said,

We don't always get along and we don't totally disagree.

Don't get me wrong. (I can feel your lecture coming through the book). I value right and wrong. Dads play a vital role in helping their kids learn the difference. Young people need to develop responsibility and make good choices, but I guarantee you, listening will overpower lecturing every time.

When you listen closely, your child may practice a line of thought on you. Without saying it out loud, he or she may be asking the question, *Dad, what do you think about this?* You may be more effective in helping your child hear the logic (or illogic) of his or her own reasoning than forcing him or her to see the brilliance of your sound thinking.

Melinda is quite bold in her words to her dad:

Dad, I want to tell you what I really want to do with my life without you interrupting me with lectures.

Melinda is seventeen. She is very close to a time when her own opinions will guide her every step. She is at the age of the release stage, but she is still trying to relate to her dad because they have never moved past the second stage of their relationship. No doubt she remains a rookie decision maker because Dad is quick to lecture and slow to listen. Granted, he may mean well. But he's driving her crazy. Melinda said,

My dad is cool but he doesn't always listen, and he decides my life for me.

Who is going to make the call when Melinda's dad is not around?

Too many children go into their teen years disconnected. Adolescence serves as an apprenticeship for adulthood, a vital transition to practice life under the guidance of a master craftsman. When a teenager should be at a point to begin interacting with the world under the protection of Dad and Mom, too many are still searching for love, acceptance, and a way to stop the pain. The readily available quantities of drugs, alcohol, sex, and other high-risk activities overwhelm the young person's search for connection. Melinda will stand as no match for such a virile competitor. Chemicals and crisis sex leave scars behind. They even take lives.

Dad, if the word *lecture* resurrects the ol' schoolteacher image from way back when, remember: Lectures create chalkdust and choke the pupils.

3. Listening Spells R-E-S-P-E-C-T

Samuel is fifteen, and he thinks his dad is *awesome* and *the greatest*. I sure hope my son, Chase, finds those words thirteen years from now if he is asked to describe me. What makes Samuel's dad receive such high accolades? He wrote,

My dad respects my opinions and will always listen to me when others don't.

Samuel's dad does not lecture; he listens. He is there when others have bailed out on Samuel. For Samuel, the cry of his heart to relate is spelled R-E-S-P-E-C-T. Aretha Franklin does not have anything on Samuel. He's already belting out the same song, and he is singing in harmony with his dad.

4. Listen to Our World

Micah is sixteen, and she's had plenty of time to see behind her dad's suit of armor. He's probably very real and very human to her. Yet listen to her description of her dad:

My dad is an awesome Christian man, and he relates to me. He goes on youth functions with me, and he even listens to my music.

Here's a dad who leaves his world of adulthood—father-focused, grown-up stuff—to join his daughter. No wonder he rates a nine on the scale. I see Micah's dad as a student of his daughter's culture.

Dad, do you want to know what makes your kids tick? Go to school with them. Next time you're jumping in the car for a drive, ask your child if you can borrow one of his tapes. You may find yourself on the receiving end of the words Micah has reserved for her dad:

Dad, you're the best dad in the world and I love you.

Now that we've heard the kids' suggestions, let me give you a few postscripts from one dad to another.

NOTES FROM ONE DAD TO ANOTHER

What about the hundreds of kids who chose to bypass my surveys? Or the young boy or girl who slipped out the back after the meeting when I said, "I'm available if any of you want to spend some time talking about your life"? How do you talk to a kid whose best means of conversation is grunting?

Listening to a Non-Talking Child

Years ago I was driving with my niece Lisa, who was a young teenager at the time and exceptionally perceptive. (Someday very soon Uncle Doug will be going to her for advice.)

She asked, "Uncle Doug, why do you like to ask open-ended questions?"

"What makes you ask that?"

She looked up at me and saw my smirk; then she smiled. I told her how I value people's opinions. Plus, I'm a curious sort, and I love to learn new stuff.

Dad, use open-ended questions to talk to a quiet kid. Don't badger. Don't become Lieutenant Columbo looking for the clue to convict your child. You might breed suspicion, and then your child will become a fugitive.

Look to your child's likes and dislikes, and use them as a bridge. Remember when you first fell in love with your child's mom? Remember how you used to court her with surprises of her favorite flower, food, or outing? Did you have to strive extra hard due to her lack of interest? What would it take today for you to "fall in love" with your child? It was enough to get you and his or her mom together; surely it will work with the offspring from the same union.

Let me offer a list of questions to give you some ideas that might help close the silence gap.

1. What does your child do with his or her free time?
2. What is his or her favorite music?
3. What is his or her favorite food?
4. What adults does he or she look up to?
5. What sports or hobbies does he or she pursue?

6. How does he or she act in a crowd of new people?
7. What classes does he or she like or do well in at school?
8. What does he or she do with his or her money?
9. What are the names and personality types of his or her two best friends?
10. What would he or she do if he or she had a whole day off to do whatever he or she wanted?

Take any one of these questions and ask it directly—or research it indirectly. Then use it as an entrée for the next time you talk with your son or daughter.

Listen to What Your Child Does Not Say

Words can be deceiving; they can provide a key to open a door, or they can exist as a smoke screen, distracting the listener from the true meaning. You don't have to be a professional to hear beyond words. Make one target your goal: Listen to your child's heart. Deeper meaning is there if you come close enough to listen and stay long enough to hear. One young person named Breanna helped us dads better understand what is going on behind her words:

Even though I don't show it or say it as well as I should, I do care about him.

In so many words, she is saying, *Don't be fooled by the masks I wear.*

LISTENING WILL NOT OPEN EVERY DOOR

Chrissy reminds us dads,
I look up to my dad a lot and ask him questions. I share my

feelings with him, and he listens and gives correct answers. But, I can't talk to him about girl stuff.

Dad, never charge in to force a child to speak about the tender parts of his or her soul. I call this the "holy of holies." Some doors are best left closed. Other doors hide very precious items. One day, if you find yourself invited into your child's inner world of fear or pain or confusion, take off your shoes and walk carefully for you are on holy ground.

Dad, your child invites you to relate to him or her. Your child cries, *Listen to me.* In the exchange you will discover the power of intimacy, when one person draws another into his or her own soul. It is a refreshing, breathtaking ride like a powerful, graceful glide across the waterscape of God's creation.

Dear Dad,

    Please listen to me. Hear what I say, and more important, what I don't say or what I am trying to say.

Love,
Your child

CHAPTER 8

Dear Dad,

Please forgive me.

Love,
Your child

PLEASE FORGIVE ME.

Dad, we get along well, and if I had a problem you could help me. I could tell you anything without you freaking out.
Kim, age fifteen

Dad, you spend a lot of time with me and talk honestly about issues with me.
Jeff, age fourteen

Erma Bombeck wisely advises, "Never lend your car to anyone to whom you have given birth."

Erma is a wise woman. Sometimes wisdom comes from practical experience. I've learned there are three steps to raising children.

Step 1.   Birth the child (vicarious but reverent and supportive from a dad's perspective).
Step 2.   Raise the child.
Step 3.   Forgive the child when step 2 is no longer possible.
Step 4.   (Optional) Return the child when step 3 is no longer possible.

With the exception of children, parenting is a wonderful experience. Often, children mess up our parenting plans. If they don't, life will. What do you and I as dads do when real life comes crashing in on our plans? Your child's courage or fear will relate in direct proportion to your action as a dad. What does your child anticipate from you when he or she brings home some news that is less than desirable? Does your child expect "the big one"? Take a moment to quiz yourself on the disaster scale.

TAKE THE QUAKE QUIZ

Rate how you would react to the following situations. Use the Richter scale from one to seven (one = mild tremor; seven = devastating quake) and finish the statement, "When my child . . ."

comes home ten minutes late for curfew. _____

comes home one hour late for curfew. _____

forgets to call home. _____

calls home from the police station. _____

brings home a stray pet. _____

brings home a stray boyfriend or girlfriend. _____

brings home a dented car . . . mine. _____

comes home with a shaved head. _____

comes home with a new earring. _____

comes home with a new earring . . . and he's a boy. _____

gets a D in class. _____

gets an F in class. _____

gets pregnant. _____

moves out to get married. _____

moves out to move in with a lover. _____

drinks alcohol under age. _____

takes drugs. _____

How did you do? Are your responses appropriate? Explosive? Forgiving? You be the judge of where you rate overall. Are your responses in some areas too explosive?

One set of parents was surprised to get the following letter from their daughter who was away at college. She wrote:

Dear Dad & Mom,

Just thought I'd drop you a note to clue you in on my plans. I've fallen in love with a guy named Jim. He quit high school after grade eleven to get married. About a year ago he got a divorce.

We've been going steady for two months and plan to get married in the fall. Until then, I've decided to move into his apartment (I think I might be pregnant).

At any rate, I dropped out of school last week, although I'd like to finish college sometime in the future.

On the next page she continued,

Mom and Dad, I just want you to know that everything I've written so far in this letter is false. None of it is true.

But Mom and Dad, it IS true that I got a C in French and flunked math. It IS true that I'm going to need some more money for my tuition payments.[1]

Did you feel the panic this dad and mom must have experienced? A failing grade in math class and a few more bucks for tuition pale in comparison. If only you and I as dads could react to all situations by saying, "Oh, is that all?"

Fifteen-year-old Kim told me she could tell her dad anything without his freaking out. On the other hand, seventeen-year-old Mitch and I talked about some of the mistakes we both made as teenagers as we sat together on the floor of a gym. He shared with me what he said he

Wouldn't dare tell my dad.

Some kids out there have what they consider to be great dads. Fourteen-year-old Kimberly is one of them. She said,

He's a great father because he listens to my problems.

Seventeen-year-old Justus is another example of a son with a fantastic dad. Why?

Dad, you're the best dad in the world because you help me with my problems. Our relationship is a ten!

What causes a child to rank his or her dad in double digits? It comes down to the response to one clear question: "What do you do when real life comes crashing in on your plans?"

It's so much easier raising children without kids around— and that's been true for centuries. Consider this gloomy analysis: "Children today are tyrants. They contradict their parents, gobble their food, and tyrannize their teachers." Sound relevant to today? Socrates said that more than two thousand years ago!

No one has invented a WD-40® to make families "friction-free." Parenting reaches the boiling point during the era I have labeled the second part of this great life drama, the dialogue. This stage begins in the preteen years around age ten and reaches full gallop by age sixteen. Kids are telling me they want to relate to their dads. They want more than just a silent partner with whom they connect.

Let me illustrate what I see as the change between Act 1 and Act 2. Brave twelve-year-olds look across a chasm connected by a flimsy, wobbly bridge. They dig down deep to muster up the courage to cross. Unless the beginning point of the bridge is well connected, the traveler will find little stability in the middle of the trip.

And regardless of the strength of the bridge, every child—*every child*—will stumble. Kids are kids. They are filled with the mythology of adolescence: the belief that any gorge is neither too deep nor too wide to cross. Many young people fall, some to their deaths. Teenagers are not small grown-ups. They are big kids who are striving to learn how to survive the heat and succeed in the world.

Fathers exist to help their children leave the oasis of connectedness on the safe side and risk the journey across to new and unknown lands. Growing up is never friction-free. Mistakes are inevitable. Fatherhood is a participatory sport that cannot be experienced by remote control from the comfort of the couch. It began with an act. It remains an active role.

The dialogue in the drama of parenting is the verbal exchange from a child to the father and back to the child. The second message from your child is *Forgive me*. Dads, our children are requesting a response from us. They are asking for a gift. Therein lies the real adventure in parenting. They are hoping for an allowance, something given freely when it is really not deserved. Whether now, in the years to come (for dads who don't have teenagers yet), or from years past for fathers who have grown adults, our kids want to know, *Dad, will you forgive me?*

Maybe your child ran at the bridge too hard and too fast. Maybe he or she carelessly skipped along and neglected to watch his or her footing. Maybe your child clung to the safe side for fear of falling. Maybe he or she got too far out and could no longer look back and call for you or listen to your guidance. Maybe your child failed. If not yet, prepare yourself, because he or she will. When your child does, the message will be, *Forgive me.*

Dad, you and I are asked to surrender. At age seventy-four, Norman Cousins wrote:

> I doubt that I have learned as much in life as a reasonably long lifetime should be expected to provide, but a few things stand out. I have learned that life is an adventure in forgiveness. Nothing clutters the soul more than remorse, resentment, recrimination. Negative feelings occupy a fearsome amount of space in the mind, blocking our perceptions, our prospects, our pleasures. Forgiveness is a gift we need to give not only to others but to ourselves, freeing us from self-punishment and enabling us to see a wider horizon in life than is possible under circumstance of guilt or grudge.[2]

Dad, it is very difficult to forgive our children and ourselves. We experience the disappointment of failed expectations, and our hearts break. We watch our kids hurt. We face our own depression or anger resulting from a battle to let go. The gift of forgiveness is an expensive present. Yet without this gift, our children will not move beyond connectedness to a growing relationship.

Many adults are unable to connect with another adult, especially intimately, because their dads never gave them the gift of forgiveness and the adult child is still waiting for it to arrive, like a ship lost at sea. At a young age, acceptance provides a foundational base of connection. But it is forgiveness that builds the tower to rise above ground level.

A child's *Forgive me* calls us ordinary dads to rise up to the extraordinary, sometimes giving beyond what we feel we may possess. Norman Cousins wrote, "Certainly nothing is more characteristic of the Deity than forgiveness."[3]

What happens when dads work with problems in the family? Let me allow a thirteen-year-old named Allie to answer the question.

My dad is the color blue.

He makes me feel our house is on solid ground.

He helps me through all of the problems that I ever had.

He's nice and teaches me a lot.

If I could tell my dad anything, I'd say, "Dad, you are the best dad in the world. I don't know what I would do without you. I would be lost in life."

When I asked kids about the word *problem*, I found a gold mine of insights. Problems exist, especially in preteens and teenagers. I want to pass on to you what I hear from kids on what works and what doesn't work for dads during the dilemmas.

KIDS SPEAK OUT ABOUT DADS DURING THE DILEMMAS

Fifteen-year-old Mark said his dad,

Tries to be a good father to me and talks with me about my problems.

Marie is the same age as Mark. She said this about herself and her dad:

We have no problems, and if we do, we work them out so then again we have no problems.

For a minute I thought I had found the first friction-free,

flawless family. Then the truth came through. Marie and her dad do have problems. They just don't let problems sit very long. They work them out.

Another young person gave his relationship with his dad a ten because,

We do a lot together and I can discuss problems with him. We can talk freely and he doesn't lecture me.

A ten, Dad . . . *ten!* Do you want to reach the top of your child's ladder? Then take a moment to look back on the responses above from Mark, Marie, and our other child-guidance counselor. What do you see?

Words like *talk, work, discuss,* and *understand.* Dad, do you want to handle the heat? Allow problems to exist. Talk about them. Strive to understand. Give your child room to fail. Help your child move across the bridge of adolescence.

I looked more closely at the last young man's comments, and I found that progression from the first phase—*I want to connect with you*—to the second phase—*I want to relate to you:*

The Statement	The Message	The Heart
We do a lot together.	*Be with me.*	Connect
We can talk freely.	*Listen to me.*	Relate
He doesn't lecture me.	*Listen to me.*	Relate
I can discuss problems.	*Forgive me.*	Relate

In *People of the Lie,* M. Scott Peck wrote, "It is not fun to fail. But it can be highly educational. . . . We probably have even more to learn from our failures than from our successes."[4]

A twelve-year-old named Lisa echoed Dr. Peck's comments about learning and growing. She said her relationship with her dad is a nine because *We share problems.* There's room to fail in her home.

What does she want to pass on to her dad?

Dad, you are a wonderful dad and you're teaching me a lot and you're making me grow up very strong and wise. I love you very much.

What dad does not want his child to grow up strong and wise? What dad wants less than a nine in a relationship with his child? What dad doesn't want to be called *wonderful?* How do we make it work?

Let's look first at what *doesn't* work so we can discard those approaches and then, at the end of this chapter, focus on what does work. To find the answers, let's go to those who know best: the kids.

WHAT RESPONSES DON'T WORK?

One student responded this way to the question, "If you could say anything to your dad, what would you say?"

Everything: my worries, problems, and dreams.

Another young person offered,

My relationship with my dad is a one. We don't talk. He deals with problems by ignoring them.

What if you could say anything to him?

I'd tell him, "Dad, I love you."

Here are two young people who desperately want to tell their dads about everything in their lives: their worries, their problems, their dreams. One of them is put off by a dad who deals with problems by ignoring them. Dad, what does *not* work with problems in the family?

Pretending. Pretending leads to a relationship at the bottom, a one. Is there hope? Dad, let failure be your teacher and teach you hope.

One of these kids offers her dad a resilient love. Your child may do the same for you.

What else doesn't work with problems in the family?

Loretta, a fourteen-year-old female, told me her relationship with her dad is a seven. Why?

We don't have much of a relationship.

What color best describes your dad?

White. My dad is a clean freak.

What would you say if you could say anything to your dad?

Dad, it would not be the end of the world if the world was a mess.

What is Loretta facing with her dad? Unrealistic expectations. Pretending and unrealistic expectations are two responses that kids tell me don't work for dads during the dilemmas.

Dad, will your child ever measure up to your standards? I'll assume you want what is best for your child. I do. I truly believe one of my kids' greatest challenges in life will be to live up to the ideals I have set for them. I have to be careful not to say, "Good job, dear, but you know, you could have done it a little bit better, faster, sharper, smarter, cleaner."

WHAT RESPONSES DO WORK?

Dad, problems work for fathers when failure becomes a teacher. What can be learned by our child when he or she fails? I find three valuable lessons passed on to our child from Professor Failure.

Lessons from Professor Failure

1. *Failure can teach humility.* Failure teaches us that we can't do something with just our own abilities. Failure reminds us we need other people. Failure communicates to the student that he or she does not know all, and that is a humble place to be.

Dad, forgiveness does not remove the teachable moment; it enhances it. Although we may forgive the mistakes or sins, the scars still remain. I sit here at my computer looking at the scar on my left hand. I remember climbing in the refrigerator-box fort my boyhood friends and I built on the front lawn of Chris MacDonald's house. In our haste, we had neglected to remove the huge staples used to clamp the box shut during shipping.

While scampering through the box, the back of my left hand caught one of the staples. Blood and tears followed. Twenty-nine years later, I'm still a little careful when it comes to messing with boxes and shipping staples. Ask me about the pain of the cut skin and I'll tell you I know it like the back of my hand. The sin is gone, but the scar long remains. It humbly reminds me far more effectively than any lecture my dad could have delivered.

In short, when kids fail and fathers forgive, young people learn that they are humble and human. A humble young person also learns two other lessons in failure: Failure teaches healing, and failure teaches hope.

2. Failure can lead to healing. Failure is painful. When failure shows us what does not work, we find a place in need of healing. Then healing can be applied to the right spot. Forgiveness of failure is the healing touch of the divine on the hurting heart of the human. Songwriting team Elton John and Bernie Taupin captured the power of that healing in "The Last Song," words a son speaks to his father when the father visits his son as he lies dying of AIDS.

As the story goes, the son is filled with fear and his only request is to be held in his father's arms, to be calmed by his dad's gentle hands. His fear gives way to freedom as he reveals the truth of the life he once hid and experiences what he doesn't expect: his father's understanding and love: "I guess I misjudged love between a father and a son," he says.[5] Within the healing comes another precious lesson learned from failure: Failure teaches hope.

3. Failure can teach hope. The child who never fails will lose the privilege of learning one of life's greatest joys: the chance to find what happens in one's very own soul when the presence of hope says, "Rise up and try again. You can overcome the fall."

I watched as Robert Schuller interviewed a young man on *The Hour of Power*. Craig MacFarlane stood strong and tall, a good-looking blond with captivating eyes. No doubt, young women were swooning. One thing about Craig made him most unique: He was blind.

Craig is an outstanding athlete, and he loves the game of golf. As an avid golfer, my interest was piqued. He talked about shooting an 89 in a recent round of golf, a score most guys like me appreciate . . . and I can see! He talked about sinking an eighty-six-foot putt by using muscle memory. He would walk from the cup to where his ball lay and use his mind to picture the break and slope of the green. He then dropped the putt from nearly one hundred feet away.

Craig also loves to snow ski. He laughed his way through stories of skiing sixty miles per hour downhill. I thought, *Are you kidding? I sweat at half that speed . . . with my eyes open.* Craig's ability to succeed focused on two dynamics: First, he began every day with what he called his "morning vitamin pill," his prayer life. Second, he learned to put his trust in people who helped him through.[6]

Craig is an incredible example of a student whose debilitating failure of sight enabled him to experience healing and growth in his soul and his mind. He was humble, and confident but not arrogant; he knew there were others with much greater abilities. Craig also spoke as a young man with hope. Tomorrow was worth facing because of what he had learned from yesterday and today.

Dad, problems can work to our advantage.

Before I address the gift of forgiveness, I can hear some dads thinking, *Are we supposed to just write off every mistake our kids make with some pie-in-the-sky, soft-hearted response? What about teaching values to our kids, you know, right and wrong?* Good questions.

Dads, the bigger question at stake is, "Can we love, accept, and forgive our children without backing their actions?" I recently asked that question to a dad who was facing his pregnant daughter's pending choice of abortion. He adamantly opposed the decision. Yet she was very seriously considering it. At her age in this country, she has every right and opportunity to choose her action regardless of her dad's or mom's opinions on abortion.

Unfortunately this dad may soon face the question, "Can I choose to love and forgive my daughter regardless of her choice?" I pointed out to this dad, "Realize your daughter came to you with a possible decision she knew you would disapprove of. Your love relationship (and past history of forgiveness) may provide her with enough courage to make a different decision." Don't disregard the failed action. Rather, focus on the formidable person. Think about the word *encourage,* which means "to instill courage in someone."

Failure grants us dads a better chance to say, "I love you in spite of what you've done" than when our kids perform the showstopping routine. Heck, everyone else is cheering, "You're the greatest" when the curtain closes. Everyone likes a star. We get lost in the crowd of admirers.

Who stands in his or her corner when the person is cut from the cast, forgets the lines, or falls during the dance? Therein lies a precious moment to present a powerful gift of love and forgiveness, a healing for today's hurt and hope in the face of tomorrow's failures.

THE GIFT OF FORGIVENESS

In May of 1981, Saint Peter's Square in Rome was the sight of one of history's most horrific events, an assassination attempt on Pope John Paul II. The pope survived the attack and continues to this day as one of the greatest leaders of our modern era.

To me his greatness does not come from his ability to rise from this life-threatening incident, although few of us could ever do the same. What stands out so clearly about the depth of this man's character is his response to this attack. Three years later Pope John Paul sat in Rome's Rebibbia Prison holding the hand of his would-be assassin, Mehmet Ali Agca. In the privacy of the prisoner's cell, the pope proclaimed a message for the whole world to hear: "I forgive you."

I believe Pope John Paul II would not credit his nobility of this historic act to his personal fortitude and depth of character. Rather, the pope has personally experienced the forgiveness of another Father through his faith in the Father's Son, Jesus. Forgiveness, although costly, is a freely offered gift. It produces life-changing results like no other relational exchange. Don't misunderstand the power of the act; the pope drew from experience, not expertise.[7]

That single act has positioned the pope as a leader among all of the world's leaders. Through the power of forgiveness and compassion, Pope John Paul II has earned the right to be heard. He has seized the listening ear of all ages as well. In 1993 in Colorado, tens of thousands of young people traveled from around the world to hear this man speak. And they listened closely to what he had to say. The pope proved what our kids are telling us: *Forgiveness draws children into relationships.*

Dad, you and I are not asking children from around the world to sit at our feet. We are looking for one child or a few children in particular to be willing to walk down the hall to be with us. How can it happen? Hear and respond to your child's message, *Forgive me.*

How do we treat our children who have caused friction, problems, and pain in our lives and the lives of our families? Take some advice from one of our leaders who exemplified hope found in failure, Abraham Lincoln. When asked how he was going to treat the rebellious Southerners who only returned to the Union of the United States because they had been defeated, Lincoln responded, "I'll treat them as if they had never been away."

In giving the gift of forgiveness, we move from dads who dictate to fathers who lead. Robert Greenleaf in his incredible work on leadership, *Servant Leadership,* had some keen insights for those of us dads leading the institution of the family. He wrote:

> The "typical" person—immature, stumbling, inept, lazy—is capable of great dedication and heroism if wisely led.
>
> The secret of institution building is to be able to weld a team of such people by lifting them up to grow taller than they would otherwise be. People grow taller when those who lead them empathize and when they are accepted for what they are, even though their performance may be judged critically in terms of what they are capable of doing.[8]

Before I finish my thoughts on forgiveness I must let you in on one last insight I've received from the kids. Here it is: *Forgiveness goes both ways—between dad and child and back again.* Kids are forgiving too. Listen.

Tamera rated her relationship with her dad a negative sixteen. But what does she have to say to him?

I forgive you.

Is Tamera alone? No way!

In only eighteen years, Sue has had incredible problems in her life. She told me,

My dad was not part of my life—he disowned me when I was thirteen because I got pregnant. He died when I was in college. He was an alcoholic and drug dealer and he had little self-respect. My sister and I were raised by my grandma because Mom and Dad were too involved in other things. I almost never saw them. I'm glad I found the family I live with now (my foster family). Their faith is strong, and their love is abundant.

Sue has survived hell over the past seven years. Thank heaven she now has a new family to help her through. What would Sue say if her dad were alive and she could talk with him today?

I forgive you with only God's help; I want to love you, and I wish we could have had a better relationship.

Another young person chose to remain anonymous but let his feelings speak loud and clear:

I understand why you're like you are. I forgive you for not being a real "dad." I don't respect you cuz you have no desire to change (for our sake).

Somehow this kid found a way to understand and forgive a dad even though he doesn't feel that dad has any desire to change.

Dad, is it time for *you* to lead the drama in the second act? Is it your turn to ask for forgiveness for the friction you've caused? In doing so, you'll learn one more insight about forgiveness: *Forgiveness is not only relational; forgiveness is transformational.* Forgiveness changes the lives of people who are willing to relate.

When I finished speaking at a conference out West, a man

in his mid-sixties approached me. He was visibly shaken as he stood crying before me. He tightly clutched the arm of his wife next to him. "Doug, I've got a request for you. You spoke today about loving and forgiving those closest to us. Please tell people wherever you go to never wait until it's too late. You see, for me, it is too late."

He stopped talking to catch his breath and wipe away the tears. Then he continued, "My son just died in a diving accident last week. We left each other's presence in an argument. We fought over stupid, little things. I was too stubborn to let go and forgive him for what he had done. That day he died, and I never had the chance to say, 'I forgive you and I love you.'"

Dad, don't wait to relate. The time is at hand.

Dear Dad,

I am human and I make mistakes. I need you when I fail. Will you still love me when I mess up? I need your forgiveness to bring me back to you.

Love,
Your child

CHAPTER 9

Dear Dad,

   Be real with me.

Love,
Your child

BE REAL WITH ME.

We talk and joke and he's real with me.
Andrea, age fifteen

*He's somewhat of a blur to me. I know nothing about his private life
or his feelings. . . . He always changes the subject.*
Anonymous

When I speak to kids about their parents, I start with the line, "Your parents are not God."

"Yeah right, Doug, thanks for the brilliant insight," they respond.

"But," I ask, "do you expect them to be? Do you let them be human?"

A hush falls over the crowd.

Many young children consider their parents to be gods, or at least godlike. As a child grows, he or she quickly learns otherwise. Yet it may not be until the dialogue phase in the preteen years that a child fully experiences the fallibility of his or her parents. Godhood may stick around a family for a decade, sometimes longer.

Dad, how about your family? Does your child know that when you go into a phone booth, you come out wearing the same clothes and twenty-five cents poorer? If asked, could your child draw up an objective list of your weaknesses and inabilities? What would your child write if you asked for a list of what you don't do very well? Do you have the guts to ask?

Dad, our kids want to see our humanity. Are you ready and willing to drop your suit of armor? Like the great Wizard of Oz, what happens when Toto gets behind our curtain of disguise and reveals nothing more than a mortal man using smoke and mirrors? Will your child be surprised?

Children, especially as they hit their midteen years, tell me they have a great need to know a real dad. Why? When young people realize they have a real dad who battles a real world and wins and loses, they are better prepared to do the same. A boy learns how to be a man by watching Dad be a man. A girls learns how to relate to a man by relating to Dad as a man.

But kids don't just want Dad to be real so they can learn how to live in a real world. Kids want more. Believe it or not, Dad, your child would like a deeper relationship with you.

Twelve-year-old Sara wanted to tell her dad,

Dad, you need to be a better father.

Ooohh, tough words. Does she expect her dad to be godlike? I'll let her speak for herself:

He's never around, and I never get a chance to really know what he's like.

How could her dad go about responding to Sara's need? He could be around and let Sara know what he's really like.

For Sara and hundreds of other kids with whom I've talked, it's that simple. They want a relationship. To relate, a dad must first connect. A refresher course reminds you and me that *Be with me* is the transition from connect to relate. Sara said, *Be around and be real while you're here.*

How do we dads encourage a child to move from the safe contact of the nearby cliff to the unknown bridge of adolescence? Take the fifth message, *Be with me,* and add one word, *real,* and you've got: *Be real with me.*

What do kids see in their dads if they do not experience the real thing? They are left with nothing but fatherhood facades:

"My father, my Zeus"
"My father, internally ill"
"My father, Mr. Plastic"

FATHERHOOD FACADES

My Father, My Zeus

The picture "My father, my Zeus" is the portrait some young people have of their dads. The picture is not necessarily a false myth. What the child sees is accurate. It is just one-sided, lacking the clay feet common to every dad I know. Zeus dads don't make up stories; they simply don't offer bits of fallen history that may tarnish their image. Zeus dads live out what one writer called, "The commandments of masculinity":

He shall not cry.
He shall not display weakness.
He shall not need affection or gentleness or warmth.
He shall be needed but not need.
He shall comfort but not desire comforting.
He shall touch but not be touched.

He shall be steel not flesh.
He shall be inviolate in his manhood.
He shall stand alone.[1]

A young man named Daniel told me about his dad who fits the Zeus category. He wrote,

My dad seems so perfect and always right but humble.

At age fourteen Daniel believes his dad does everything, maybe even walks on water (but he jokingly tells you he knows where the rocks are). I can't leap to conclusions. Daniel's dad may be very honest and his son, Daniel, may choose to listen selectively.

You and I both know from our relationships with our own dads that Daniel's father is going to fall from his pedestal. I hope for Daniel's sake his dad is the one to deliver the news. For, you see, a good dad encourages his child to believe in him; a great dad encourages his child to relate to him. Godlike dads are very difficult to approach.

Dad, battle the Zeus syndrome. If you buy into the myth, you are likely to spend the rest of history carrying the world on your shoulders.

Zeus dads are not the only unreal fathers. Some dads work diligently to hide all that is inside.

My Father, Internally Ill

Some dads are men suffering from internal pain, and they will not let anyone know of their trauma. "I can handle it" is this dad's rallying cry.

Sixteen-year-old Ann can see right into her dad, but he doesn't let on. She said,

He is like the color brown. I don't know my dad very well. He has a lot of pain.

Dad, how are your health and well-being? Are there secrets hidden in the inner workings of your soul? If your child, spouse, or friend had the diagnostic tool to scope your inner heart, what condition would be revealed in it?

If you were to die soon, what six people would you want to carry your coffin? I imagine every one of us could rattle off a list of a half-dozen friends or family members who would lend a hand.

Now, if you were (are) really hurting, what two people would you ask to carry your stretcher? Would your child be one of your stretcher bearers? Or would your child be surprised to discover that you were sick?

Roxanne is sixteen years old. She described her dad as the color black. She said,

He's kind of a secret, I don't know him really. We've met but I don't know him.

What's dad like inside? No clue. Is he all right and healthy or lost and hurting? I can't tell. Too many dads could pass away tomorrow from internal physical or emotional pain and leave their families in shock.

Other dads may not be dying inside, but you can't differentiate them from the mannequin in the store window. They appear to be Disney's latest imagineering break-through: the plastic dad.

My Father, Mr. Plastic

A Japanese proverb states: "One cannot tell what passes through the heart of a man by the look on his face."[2] The third type of unreal dad is a normal, everyday dad. He is not a Father Zeus. He does not fit the bill of the dad who can do all. Nor is he burying pain held deep inside his soul.

No, Mr. Plastic fits the mold. Whenever you need him, he's there. He's the faithful provider. He doesn't run the race like Hermes, but he tries his best. He's well known for clichés such as, "Keep a stiff upper lip" and "Big boys don't cry." He'll say, "We'll get them tomorrow," even though his son or daughter's Little League team is the worst in town, with game after game called on account of embarrassment. Coach Plastic can't hit a home run, but he can sure cheer a child into thinking the child can, even if he or she is terrible.

You can never quite tell what's going through Mr. Plastic's heart by the look on his face. What makes kids so indifferent to the Mr. Plastic dad? Young people are desperately looking to counterbalance the fake, superficial world in which we live; they want authenticity.[3] They have been ripped off before, both personally and publicly.

A few years ago, pop music took some hard raps (pun intended) for some performers' false representation at live concerts. The ordeal rippled into politics and business circles. Two New Jersey state assemblymen, Neil Cohen and Joe Mecca, even sponsored a bill requiring performers to announce before their concerts whether they would sing live or lip-sync to recorded music.[4] Carl Freed, executive director of the North American Concert Promoters Association, agreed with the spirit of the bill, but his comment was, "I think the bill is a little far-fetched. There's got to be a compromise."[5]

Wait a minute! Isn't the reason the music industry finds itself in this situation due to compromise—a drop in the standards of quality for today's performers? Freed stated that the audience would "lose the ability to suspend disbelief."[6] What kind of hogwash is that? Kids are getting ripped off by performers who only pretend to sing. It's called plastic.

It is even more noteworthy to read how Milli Vanilli and New Kids on the Block used tapes for as many as half of their concerts. An article in the *Wall Street Journal* stated, "Agents for the groups didn't return phone calls."[7] Is that any surprise? New Kids on the Block were created as a prefab marketing scheme designed by recording gurus. Granted, the group's incredible success demonstrated their prowess in the music marketplace. Forget the idea of a garage band of musicians working by day and singing by night in gyms and local clubs striving for the big break. These musicians are all plastic.

The story gets even better. The article stated, "But such precision acts [New Kids and Milli Vanilli] can backfire. On tour last summer, *Billboard* reports, the group Milli Vanilli walked off the stage after a malfunction stopped its vocals. Minutes later, the band played on, but no one was on stage."

Then the biggest news hit later in the season. Milli Vanilli did not and could not sing. The group members could dance, but the voices behind the moves belonged to other people's bodies! They had received a 1990 Grammy award for best new artist for something they never were.

They sold ten million copies of their album! Let the irony continue. The name of their album was "Girl, You Know It's True." Our kids have been had by two plastic dancers in a world of synthetic record executives. When asked why they did what they did, Rob Pilatus of Milli Vanilli said, "We just wanted to live life the American way."[8]

Maybe I could secure a financier to help me launch my new line of background vocals called:

Daddy Tracks®

This group would be for all you dads who have the right look, the right moves but you just need the right words to win over your child's affection and dedication. Guaranteed to earn you the Father of the Year award.

Dad, our young people have been burned one time too many. Many of their heroes in the music, sports, and film world are blown-up caricatures. Their real lives are 180 degrees opposite of the people they portray on the stage, field, or screen.

Don't let our kids find the same plastic man at home. They don't want a dad who looks and plays the part. They are searching for an authentic, real dad. They can handle a dad who can't handle everything. Will you help your child find the real thing?

One young person told me of his plastic dad:

My dad is somewhat of a blur to me. I know nothing about his private life or his feelings. . . . He always changes the subject. Our relationship is a seven. It's above average because we've never fought and he always provides for my needs. But I feel like I really don't know him very well.

This dad is not bad. He provides for his child's needs. Their relationship is neither poor nor average, it's above average. What gives? The young man is looking for more than just a dad who is present. He wants a relationship. I'm guessing he would pass up a plastic band in concert to have a chance to be with a real dad—struggles, joys, concerns, and all.

Dad, kids want us to be real. They don't want Zeus; they can read about him in school. They prefer not to visit you in the hospital with their first words being, "I didn't even know you were sick." They don't want a plastic dad who never misses a beat. They will take us as we are—the good, the bad, and the ugly. Are you and I willing to show them the real dad behind the curtain?

If you say yes, read on. Here are the advantages the kids saw to having a real dad.

Five Benefits of a Real Dad

Real dads empower their kids' forgiveness. Dad, adding a "real" quality to your relationship with your child will provide a catalyst to spark deeper exchanges of the heart. Frankly put, the more our kids know about us, the more opportunities they will have to forgive us.

One teenager wanted to let her dad know,

I know you do things I wouldn't approve of, but I love you no matter what and I'd rather talk about it than wonder. I'd tell you how much I want you to be with me.

Another young person said,

It doesn't matter what you have done in the past. All that matters is that I love you with all my heart and I want to start again. You're great but I don't understand you. There is a wall between us.

Dad, is it time to tear down the wall? I found hundreds of kids who want to love, forgive, and relate to their dads. Kids are willing to start over. Realness will serve as a launching pad for the rocket of forgiveness to send your relationship with your child soaring.

Real dads help kids love Dad and be needed by him. The internally ill dad needs healing. The physician on call could very likely be right down the hall. I have found tremendous medicinal power in children. They believe, they love, they trust, they laugh, and they do many things us grown-up men need to relearn to find health.

Donna, age thirteen, comes from a broken home. She sees her dad's pain, and she wrote,

My parents are divorced and they don't get along. My dad and I are not really opening up to each other.

What if her dad let her in on the struggles he is facing with this new way of life? I'm not asking him to give her all the nitty-gritty details. Divorce is very messy. Kids don't need to know it all. (I'll talk about that later in this chapter when we discuss, "When real is too real.") I mean sharing thoughts, fears, and confusion.

What could happen? First, Dad will find love from Donna. She might react if he blames Mom and gets nasty. But if he stays in the realm of his own feelings, I'm willing to bet Donna will hear his heart and respond tenderly. Second, Dad will show esteem for Donna by allowing her to help him. Remember, kids care about our pain, and they want to heal that hurt. In doing so, kids feel needed and appreciated. Dad, we can give our kids great gifts by receiving their love as well as giving them our love.

Harris Barton knows the power of giving love to his dad. Barton is an offensive tackle for the San Francisco 49ers. He's spent the past seven years protecting Joe Montana and Steve Young. He is an athlete, a scholar, and an all-star on the National Football League's strongest team.

Several years ago, when Barton was ready to quit football during his sophomore year at the University of North Carolina, his dad, Paul Barton, had encouraged him to finish the season. Harris said, "I remember calling home, telling him I didn't like football and wanted to come home. He didn't like football either, but he told me he didn't want me home. He told me that I had made a commitment, and that I had to go back and apologize to the coach and at least finish the season."

Barton took his dad's advice. He was a first-round draft choice and ended up playing on two Super Bowl championship teams.

Harris could always take the hit until his father found out he had incurable brain cancer and the doctors said he only had eighteen months to live. Where was the coach or playbook to help Harris Barton handle this blitz? When the time came for Harris to give his dad a birthday gift in November, he decided to send a gift of his love and caring in person.

While other teammates were on the West Coast practicing, Barton was in Atlanta helping his dad brush his teeth and button his shirts. He told his dad that no matter what, he would always be there for him. Harris then went out and played an incredible game in possibly his best season ever as the 49ers won their fifth game in a row.

That season was a tough challenge as Barton's dad fought the disease. Harris's schedule was cramped time and time again, forcing him to miss practices. Yet the 49er offensive coach said, "Harris is having as good of a year as he has ever had, and I wonder if it isn't because he is not so worried about the game, but doing other things he is supposed to do."

The focus of such a talented football player is normally on the Pro Bowl. But for Harris Barton, a trip to the bowl is secondary to his top priority. He said, "It's funny, but I've spent the last twelve years focused only on trying to be a great football player. Now all I want to be is a great son."

Football took a backseat when Barton's dad was diagnosed with cancer. That season the United Way filmed a commercial that showed Harris and his dad walking through the woods. In the film, Harris holds his dad's hand and says, "I want you to meet my greatest fan, my greatest coach, my best friend—my dad." His dad struggled with the words, but managed to say, "Harris, you, too, have been my best friend."

Mario Pellegrini, executive producer of the United Way commercial series, said, "It was one of those commercials that was so real, we just let them tell their story. They really are a special father and son."

Harris said, "When it comes to my family, football is on the back burner. . . . People should appreciate their parents while they still have them. Appreciate them now."[9]

There is tremendous power when a child has the chance to serve his or her dad. Paul Barton needed his son. His son responded to help his father. In doing so, Harris Barton became one of the best offensive tackles in the league that year, both on and off the field. If it came to protecting me in the blitz of life, I'd give anything to have a son like Harris on my front line. Good quarterbacks know they need great lineman. Dad, who's on your team? Can you play the game alone?

Real dads help kids learn how to fail. When a dad is real with his child, especially during the times when the dad has failed, he gives his child a powerful life lesson that might have taken the child decades to learn on his or her own. I truly believe if I can help my kids fail successfully, they can do anything. For anything is easier than failing.

After Thomas Edison's seven-hundreth attempt to invent the electric light, legend has it that he was asked by a reporter, "How does it feel to have failed seven hundred times?" Edison responded, "I have not failed seven hundred times. I have not failed once. I have succeeded in proving that those seven hundred ways will not work. When I have eliminated the ways that will not work, I will find the way that will work."

Is failure the goal? Not at all. Watching a dad experience and survive failure not only teaches his child how to fail successfully, it also teaches the child to take risks. Kids who never see their dads trip and fall may never run for fear of "doing something my dad would never do." It took Edison hundreds of tries before the light went on. Each failure teaches our children what not to do next time. Eventually, they will succeed and be the wiser still.

Real dads help kids experiment with intimacy. Intimacy is a nakedness between two people that leaves nothing uncovered. In our modern day, we often reduce intimacy to the act of sex, but intimacy is much more than a mere physical act. Intimacy is the exchange of the heart between two people. Too many young people are charging into physical intimacy with no understanding or experience in the art of true intimacy. They rush in, experience a moment's closeness, and then leave all the more pained.

Dad, when you are real with your child, you teach your child how to handle another person during tender times. The honest conversations between a dad and child will remove the threat of future vulnerable dialogues, strong feelings, and awkward moments. Our realness can help our children practice relating at a deeper level than what I call "cute, fun, and popular," the bulk of conversation in today's world. Being real teaches kids how to grow deeper in relationships.

Real dads launch the message, **Trust Me.** The next message to be heard from our kids after *Be real with me* is *Trust me.* It is the beginning of the final phase of the relationship—the epilogue—which proclaims a new cry of the heart: release. The existence of realness between a father and child provides a transition to the next vital stage in your child's growing up. It is a growth point when a child realizes Dad trusts him or her with something more than the car, money, or time after dark.

When the child realizes Dad is trusting him or her with feelings, hopes, dreams, and hurts, the child will rise to a new level of trustworthiness. In essence Dad says, "I trust you enough to share me with you. Trusting you with the car shrinks by comparison. I can fix a dented car more easily than a smashed heart."

Dad, do you want your child to grow up? Trust is a vital ingredient, and a depth of realness is the harbor from which the child will sail.

The cost of your investment will pay off nicely in these six tangible benefits. If you are persuaded to take that step into reality, your next question will be, "How do I go about being real or more real with my child?"

HOW TO TAKE OFF THE MASK

What will it take for us dads to gain realness in our relationships? I suggest that we set out with these four compass points guiding our journey: learning, language, location, and length.

Learning

Dad, you can't share what you don't possess. The first step in being real with others is being real with yourself. Stop, look in the mirror of your life, and find what's really there.

One young man told me his relationship with his dad is a three. Why?

He's not in touch with his own problems and issues, so our relationship has no real depth.

This book is not just about other kids' comments on their dads. It's a gentle (and not so gentle) prodding for you to ask for your child's input on your role as a dad. The first step in finding the blessing of being real is learning who you are and who you are not. Begin as a student of yourself and your family. Then you can start sharing what you find.

Language

The next compass point focuses on your choice of language. You can't share what you can't say. How important is language? One young Asian teenager told me,

We don't really communicate that much. He speaks Korean; I speak English.

This scenario unveils what is often hidden in today's parent-child relationships, the two generations are speaking different languages. I've talked with many kids who come from a cultural background that is different from their folks'. What does it take for effective communication? Mutual commitment and investment. In this case, the child needs to learn Korean, and the parent needs to learn English.

Dad, words are not as important as the message of the heart. But, don't move so quickly that your child gets lost in the language. Look for the right words.

If you share your anger, what picture comes to mind for your child? Does your child think *Hurt? Frustration? Fear? Injustice?* Use words economically in tender times. CNN news anchor Bernard Shaw learned the value of words. "My father taught me . . . words, once spoken, cannot be recalled. I cherish words and don't use them recklessly."[10] Take advice from a man who has made a career of speaking. Avoid a shotgun approach to sharing. One word may be all your child needs to buy in.

I've picked up a few other linguistic insights during a career talking with kids:

Speak in pictures. Think of images your child would best understand. If he or she understands computers, explain that your hard drive just crashed if you're feeling depressed. If he or she is a sound-system buff and you are really angry, say you think you just blew your woofer and your tweeter is humming. The kid will get the picture.

Speak in the first person. During real times, I advise people to drop the words *you, we,* and *they.* When you're sharing about you, talk *I.* It communicates clearly, disarms, and is less threatening than *you.* Kids shut down when *you* talks come up; they start thinking *lecture.*

Speak the truth. Kids see through smoke. Don't try to pull one over on them. Their instincts tell them to wall up or run whenever an adult starts playing head games. If you feel you've reached a point you don't want to cross, be honest. Don't try to look for excuses like, "I don't think you can handle what I might say." Be real about not being more real. Kids will respect that.

Now let me point out a third directional so you don't get lost in your journey in realness: the location of your heart-to-heart talk.

Location

The importance of location was reinforced by Debra, age fifteen:

I wish my dad and I could get to know each other in a neutral atmosphere where no one is mad or accusing one another. I miss our relationship when I was younger. We used to be close.

Dad, where's the best place for you to have heart-to-heart talks with your child? For Debra, it sounds like home is more of a battleground than safe haven. Dad, what positive place brings you back to a time when your child was younger? The playground swing set? The baseball diamond? Walking on the beach? The ol' fishin' hole? What if you and your child revisited a favorite haunt? Or what about creating a new place that's just for you and your child? The setting can have a strong influence on the exchange. For some dads and kids, riding in the car is the best place for talking.

Keep in mind the public or private nature of the location and use it to your benefit. A public restaurant may be too threatening for a heart-to-heart exchange, but then again, I've recommended that some families go to a public place to keep behavior and volume civil.

The final compass point for your trip into realness is the length of your stay.

Length

Sojourners beware! Don't travel farther than you're willing to hike. If you are new at climbing, don't pick a trail ten miles long and expect to make it to the top. To keep your child interested in the dialogue, leave him or her asking for more.

A few other words of coaching: Don't push, pull, or probe. You and I can't force this kind of heart-to-heart conversation as we would do if we were trying to close a deal or complete a project. Kim is seventeen years old, and she told me about how tough it is for her and her dad to get close, even more so after the divorce. Kim said,

When we talk it's awkward. I don't live with him, and I don't know him well.

Also seventeen, Nancy is starting over with her stepdad. She said,

It's taken awhile to figure out how to have a relationship with him. I don't know my real dad very well.

Dad, growth takes time. Let the length of the relationship be long enough to provide plenty of opportunities to be together, be real, and be close. But go only as far as you feel comfortable. Let the extra stuff pile up on tomorrow's calendar.

Is there ever a time when real is too real? Yes. Although it's difficult to make blanket statements, let me offer some words on the topic of discernment.

WHEN IS REAL TOO REAL?

Dad, what level of risk can you live with? Harvey MacKay offers some business leadership insight that can be applied to our world of fatherhood. He stated, "Successful traders and successful investors both will tell you that their single most important asset is self-knowledge, not stock knowledge. They know themselves well enough to understand the level of risk they can live with."[11]

Your self-knowledge and your knowledge of your child will be the most important factors in determining your honesty in sharing. Let me say this much: Kids don't necessarily need to know everything about you or get answers to everything they ask. Do you have to tell a fourteen-year-old about all the mistakes you made with drugs, alcohol, sex, and the like when you were a teenager? Do you and I need to let our kids know the intricacies of our relationship with their mother? A bold yes may be naive or inappropriate. Teenagers are not adults. And they can only progress to their level of maturity. Think of it this way: Regardless of a fourteen-year-old's perception of his or her maturity, he or she has to be sixteen to drive legally.

Dad, if your gut tells you to hesitate on what you share, listen to your intuition. You have to live with the child. Try to distinguish between your discernment and your fear. Know that it is all right for a dad to say, "I've made mistakes that I'm not proud of. I prefer to not give all the details, but I know what it is to struggle in these areas."

C. S. Lewis's attempts to break through the artificiality of talk with his dad ended in dismal failure—"shipwrecked on the old rock."[12] Miraculously, from an impoverished world devoid of a valuable conversation with his dad, C. S. Lewis became one of the twentieth century's finest artists of eloquence and imagery with words. He captured the essence of this chapter in a scene from his book, *The Lion, The Witch, and The Wardrobe* in which Susan and Lucy watch in the night as the great and powerful lion, Aslan, walks off into the woods by himself. Aslan's heart was heavy as he faced the triumph of the evil witch and his pending death on the great Stone Table.

Aslan led them up the steep slope out of the river valley. . . . He looked somehow different from the Aslan they knew. His tail and his head hung low and he walked slowly as if he were very, very tired. Then, when they were crossing a wide open place where there were no shadows for them to hide in, he stopped and looked around. It was no good trying to run away so they came toward him. When they were closer he said, "Oh children, children, why are you following me?"

"We couldn't sleep," said Lucy and then felt sure that she need say no more and that Aslan knew all they had been thinking.

"Please may we come with you—wherever you're going?" said Susan.

"Well," said Aslan and seemed to be thinking. Then he said, "I should be glad of company tonight. Yes, you may come, if you will promise to stop when I tell you, and after that leave me to go on alone."

"Oh, thank you, thank you. And we will," said the two girls.

Forward they went again and one of the girls walked on each side of the Lion. But how slowly he walked! And his great, royal head drooped so that his nose nearly touched the grass. Presently he stumbled and gave a low moan.

"Aslan, Dear Aslan!" said Lucy, "what is wrong? Can't you tell us?"

"Are you ill, dear Aslan?" asked Susan.

"No," said Aslan. "I am sad and lonely. Lay your hands on my mane so that I can feel you are there and let us walk like that."

And so the girls did what they would never have dared to do without his permission but what they had longed to do ever since they first saw him—buried their cold hands in the beautiful sea of fur and stroked it and, so doing, walked with him.[13]

Dad, your child wants to walk with you through life. Showing him or her your low times of sadness and loneliness will take your relationship to new heights. You will also grant your child an endearing, relational love to carry on to the third and final act in this life drama of growing up: the epilogue. Listen closely, Dad, and you will hear the next cry of your child's heart—release.

Dad, your child would like your permission to put a small hand in your great mane and walk with you.

> *Dear Dad,*
>
> *I want to know the real you. Please don't pretend, hide, or stay away. Just be you because I love you and I can learn from your struggles.*
>
> *Love,*
> *Your child*

PART

FOUR

THE
KIDS'
EPILOGUE:

Release me.

WHAT KIDS SAY . . .

Dad, I love you, and one day I will make you very proud of me when I grow up.
Anonymous

Dad, lighten up. Don't worry so much.
Krista, age fifteen

WHAT KIDS MEAN . . .

Trust me.

Leave me alone.

WHAT KIDS NEED . . .

A dad who trusts his kids to grow up on their own.

A dad who stays close but lets go.

CHAPTER 10

Dear Dad,

Trust me.

Love,
Your child

TRUST ME.

Dad, you need to relax and understand one important thing—I am growing up.
Angie, age sixteen

Dad, don't spend life worrying about me.
Corrine, age fourteen

Dad, please support my goals, be proud of me, and don't change me.
Linda, age sixteen

The ringing phone startled me awake. You know the feeling. When the phone rings in the middle of the night, you're challenged to connect your brain, your body, and your mouth at the same time.

"Uh-huh . . . right, no, no . . . I'm awake." Why do we try to sound so alert when we are awakened by a phone call? (Sure, I'm always sharp and responsive at one in the morning!)

The young man's voice on the other end of the phone finally brought me out of dreamland and into reality. "Doug, this is Marcus. I need some help." Marcus was a kid in my youth group who was living with his stepdad and mom. "Doug, I'm at the Circle K, and my car broke down. Can you come get me?"

By this time I had remembered the important things: My

name is Doug, I did know a kid named Marcus, I think I know where the Circle K is located . . .

"What's going on, Marcus?" I probed. "What are you doing at the Circle K?"

I was not his dad, but I did think I had the right to ask since I had just donated my precious sleep, a pounding heart, and a bucket load of adrenaline to this teenager.

"Well . . ." He began building his case. "You see, the car we were driving broke down. I need a ride back home, and I didn't want to wake my folks."

Car? The syrup-like blood in my veins was starting to flow again, and oxygen was finally making its way to my brain. "Marcus, you can't drive."

"I know. I'm glad the cop never asked for my license."

"Cop? What cop? Are you in trouble?" I asked. Smart question. A thirteen-year-old boy calls me in the middle of the night because his parents don't know he is out with no transportation back home since the vehicle he was illegally driving broke down, and the police officer never asked him for a license he did not have. Trouble? Stupid inquiry, but then again, who makes sense in the middle of the night?

"Tell me where you are, and I'll come get you."

I was young back then. I would respond differently now. When Marcus called, my first instinct as a rookie youth worker, barely a few years removed from the sophomoric stunts common to guys like Marcus, was to jump in and help the kid. Part of my motive was to get a young man off the streets. I also wanted a person to need my help.

Marcus made it home safely. He climbed in his window

and promised me he would talk it over with his folks in the morning. I didn't even want to ask how he would get the car home. I'd let him figure out that problem on his own.

I saw Marcus a few weeks later at a youth-group meeting. He told me he had worked out the problem and his parents let him off lightly. He owed that much to me. I made their job easy.

If Marcus called today, I would still answer the phone in a stupor. My experience has not diminished my middle-of-the-night fog. It's still dense. Yet my response to Marcus would be much clearer. Why? First, because these days my drive to be needed is finding many more outlets than I can accommodate. Second, because I've learned the best way to assist kids in growing up is to help their parents help them grow up.

Unless Marcus was heading back to a home of abuse, I'd give him my telephone credit card number and tell him to call his parents. My compassion has not dropped; my wisdom has increased. The sooner young people learn to handle the consequences of their decisions, the sooner they grow up. I made Marcus's learning opportunity less opportune. Much as if I had written his term paper for him, I softened the blow of this young man's failing his late-night driver's education class.

The message kids want their dads to hear is loud and clear: *Trust me.* Marcus intuitively knew it would have been more difficult to rally a positive response to this message with a "driving without a license" citation on his record.

Life, Dad, is a phone call. Either you just got one, you're in the middle of one now, or the phone is about to ring. The Marcuses of your life are on the line for you.

It's time to talk about the teaching-values side of the decisions kids make in their lives. Here we go. I hear young person after young person stating a very clear message: *Trust me*. Dad, you and I need to respond to that inquiry. Will we trust our children?

Cori, a young woman of seventeen, told me about her relationship with her dad. She gave it a seven. What's going on with you and your dad, Cori?

My dad is just scared of me growing up.

I can empathize with Cori's dad. I, too, am fearful of letting my kids grow up. What freedoms and opportunities will we grant them as they grow up? How do we respond when our trust is matched by a crisis or a change in the plan? I hope the following case study will help you and I practice our way through the maze of raising children.

THE CURFEW CASE

Pretend you have just been approached by your child with the question, "Dad, can I stay out until 2 A.M.?" Let me set the stage. The current curfew is 11 P.M. It is a weekend with no school the next day. Your child is a female like Cori. Now, what do you say?

I can see three possible roles you or I could take in this case: dictator, philanthropist, or parent. Let's review our options one at a time:

The Dictator

"No way! Curfew is at 11 P.M. Cori, you know good and well what time you are supposed to be in. Why do you question the rules?"

(Of course, her curfew was set when she turned sixteen as a sophomore in high school. She is now a senior with a good track record. She is not asking to change the rule, just adjust it for this one night. . . . Still, it's the principle of the thing!)

"Cori, I said no, and that's final!"

The Philanthropist

"Honey, if you think you can stay out until 2 A.M., that is OK with me. If that's what you want, I'll support you. I trust you implicitly."

The Parent

"Cori, let me hear you clearly: You want to stay out later tonight, three hours past your normal curfew. Do you mind helping me understand what's involved here? I'd like to ask a few questions." Then you might ask:

- "Why is it important for you to be out three hours later?"
- "Where will you be during that time?"
- "Who will be with you?"
- "Will there be any adult supervision?"
- "What consequences can we build into the agreement if you're late?"
- "How have you been in honoring your normal curfew time?"
- "When do you need to know my answer?"

By this time Cori may be screaming. She was praying for

a clean "yes," anticipating a possible "yes, but," and dreading a "no." She was prepared to appeal your decision.

Here's the downside of taking the role of a parent over dictator or philanthropist. Parenting takes time. Parenting shares decision making. Parenting does not always make you popular like philanthropy does. Parenting is seldom as clear or as easy as dictatorial rule.

Here's the upside of choosing to parent—the question, and therefore the child, is taken seriously. Parenting costs time but invests value. When we hear the child's *Trust me* message, we dads will move the child into his or her third and final cry of the heart, *Release me*. Dad, welcome to life's drama, Act 3: The Epilogue.

THE THIRD CRY OF THE HEART

The third cry of a young person's heart is one word: *release*. Webster's dictionary defines release as, "To set free from confinement or restraint; to let go of; an authoritative discharge; to give up."

Although some children begin the cry of release at a younger age, I believe this does not become a full-heart cry until the passage years of sixteen to eighteen. Those screaming for release prior to their middle-teen years often suffer from a disconnected relationship pained by hurt and anger. Or their cry to relate in the second phase of the father-child life drama was never heard. These kids are stuck in Act 2. For these young teens, the dialogue of listening, forgiveness, and realness is missing or underdeveloped because of an absent father. The premature cry of release is a defense mechanism, driving the child out of the home to find the connection and/or relating he or she desperately needs.

Some young people also linger in the epilogue beyond their teen years, causing latent or delayed release to occur. Dad can be a main contributor to an extension of Act 3 with his inability to hear, heed, and encourage the final message of *Trust me*.

This chapter deals with what I consider to be the most gruesome function of parenting: letting go of our kids. The task is tough. But what is the alternative? An eternal child stuck in perpetual adolescence. Observe the adults in your life. You won't have to look far to find adults who are immature young people inside an adult shell. It's funny (weird funny, not ha-ha funny); our society is made up of teenagers desperately trying to grow up and adults desperately striving to stay young. Many young people eventually discover the road they so eagerly wanted to travel is the last place they want to be.

I am very aware of the risk of letting go too soon. We've talked about how life hurts. What dad wants to cast his child into the heat prematurely? Today's culture is an adversary, not an ally, for us dads. But what if we don't let go or let go too late? I believe parents are more responsible for the pain of the transition from childhood to adolescence than children are. Children want to experience God's natural design for maturing. We dads either get in the way or get lost along the way.

If we could find him, I think Aimee's dad would give us some winning coaching in helping kids grow up. Just ask Aimee. I did. She said,

My dad doesn't treat me like I'm in preschool and gives me room to grow.

Aimee is sixteen years old, so she is full stride into Act 3 and looking for release. And her dad is there to deliver. In turn, Aimee has rated her relationship with her dad an eleven. She blew the lid right off the scale! For your information, Aimee's dad is one of only two dads who ranked an eleven out of the more than fifteen hundred people I talked with. The other lucky dad has an eleven-year-old son named Xavier. What's the scoop on Xavier's dad? Xavier colors him black because *God made him that way.* (I love the literal nature of preteens.)

What makes the relationship an eleven?

My dad is fun!

Anything you want to pass on to your dad, Xavier?

I love you.

With hopes of following in Xavier's and Aimee's dads' footsteps, let's march on with a look at the three steps to release: ready, aim, and fire!

Ready

Bea is fifteen years old and on the threshold of the third act, the epilogue. She really wants to grow up, much like every other kid does. She's not quite sure how to go about it, but her dad is not the one she'll go to for the training.

Bea told me,

I wish he could control what he says because he hurts others without thinking, and I wish I could ask him things concerning my growing up without hesitation. I don't talk about everything with him because I'm scared to ask him questions concerning a subject that I know will get him mad.

Bea wants to grow up but her fear of her dad holds her back. At fifteen she wants and needs to talk. But he won't listen. He gets mad. His lack of response to the messages of the first two acts—connect and relate—is holding her in a disconnected relationship.

Gina is more direct. She simply says,

Dad, let me grow up.

At the beginning of this chapter, Angie told her dad, *Dad, you need to relax and understand one important thing—I'm growing up.*

How old is Angie? Sixteen. What happens around that age? Curtain call for the third act, release.

She sounds so final, so deliberate, doesn't she? Does it strike you as odd that a sixteen-year-old is telling the adult dad what needs to happen next? Dad, kids have a message, *Trust me,* because they are growing up. Our role is to be ready.

By George. Have you ever heard of a guy named George Wythe? I didn't think so. He lived more than two hundred years ago. What George Wythe did isn't nearly as vital as who he influenced. George was a signer of the Declaration of Independence and a member of the Constitutional Convention. Like all of the country's founding fathers, Wythe contributed to a revolution and the phenomenon of a new sociopolitical system that has never been matched since. Yet his greatest role was as the mentor of one of America's greatest leaders, Thomas

Jefferson, not as a political architect and statesman. When this statesman received guidance by George, we received a country by Thomas.

Dad, consider yourself a founding father. Your role is not just designing and signing. Your part is to ready your child to make his or her contribution. Students of history will not recall George Wythe, but everyone who ever spent one hour in an American history class knows Thomas Jefferson, who wrote the Declaration of Independence. His résumé is lengthy and diverse. He was our nation's third president and served two terms. He was a diplomat, statesman, writer, social revolutionist, scientist, musician, paleontologist, inventor, educator, farmer . . . and the list continues. His dad must have been pleased. Upon his inauguration I can imagine in the crowd another proud man, this one named George, to whom Jefferson looked and said "thank you" with a smile. By George, Jefferson was prepared to influence history.

I have my own "by George" experience. There was a man born in the first quarter of this century you won't know by name. He also has a résumé full of talent and tasks, but for me, his greatest contribution to modern history was not what he did, but who he influenced. His name is also George; he is my father, George Calvin Webster. Allow me to pass on fifteen qualities that contributed to my own declaration of independence—by George:

- A conservative nature to secure and preserve life
- A Protestant work ethic to honor my responsibilities
- The beauty of a tee shot with a slight draw

- The practice of "a dollar saved is a dollar earned"
- The inner workings of an engine
- The necessity of a well-maintained piece of machinery
- The tall importance of truth
- The insignificance of a man's small stature when he thinks big
- The value of critical thinking and thorough research
- An ability—no, a necessity—to persevere
- Loyalty to children through thick and thin, pain and pleasure
- A love for the full game of baseball or the delight of just playing catch
- An appreciation of a computer
- Enjoyment of a sporting event accompanied by a nap on the couch
- Toasted bread on my sandwich

My relationship with my dad is far from ideal. You've heard me say it took twenty-one years and a brush with death to prompt us to say, "I love you." But much of who I am, I am by George, and I am grateful.

Middle- to late-teenage youths are searching for a mentor, not a master to help them grow up. They are ready to sign a declaration of independence. Your teen is looking to you, Dad, and by George, you'll do. We dads can ready our kids to take on the world and possibly make history.

One man said his dad proved the difference for him. Dr. Bernie Siegel, author of *Love, Medicine, and Miracles,* wrote:

My father had faith in me and loved me. Maybe you don't exactly learn from that, but it allows you to take on the world. Robert Frost said, "Home is a place that when you go there they have to let you in." I grew up knowing I was accepted and loved, and that made an incredible difference.[1]

Here's a personal example of a dad's role to ready a child. My father-in-law was lucky enough to escort his daughter, my wife, as the homecoming queen. (Of course, it was before she was my wife, but I like to ride on his coattails and gather some esteem from the event.) Even still, when it came down to the inaugural dance, Dad stepped aside. It was another time of release for Bob Glick in his role as a dad. In the competition of Dad versus Date, sorry Dad, the date wins. Not many years later, Bob found himself escorting his daughter again, this time down the center aisle of a church. In his one phrase, "Her mother and I do," he released his daughter into my care. He stepped aside to become the second most important man in his daughter's life. For that I am forever grateful.

Once we dads help our children get ready for life, it is time to turn to the next step: aim.

Aim

Chuck Colson, a former adviser to President Richard Nixon, served time in prison for his criminal acts in Watergate. Yet he has become one of the nation's foremost critical thinkers on our sociopolitical system through his writing. He's also a respected authority on the reform of prisons through Prison Fellowship.[2]

Colson offers clarity to help us dads aim for the target:

Parents take small self-centered monsters who spend much of their time screaming defiantly and hurling peas on the carpet and teach them to share, to wait their turn, respect others' property. These lessons translate into respect for others, self-restraining, obedience to law—in short, into the virtues of individual character that are vital to a society's survival.[3]

Colson has pegged the truth. Our hope is to end up with potty-trained contributors to society who have exceptional oral hygiene. I like to call the pursuit of our aim "parenting on purpose."

I think of bows and arrows when I picture parenting.[4] The parent is the bow, and the child is the arrow. As a parent, you do the best you can to shape your child's guiding feathers, aim him or her in the right direction, and give him or her the fire power that's needed. Once the arrow leaves the bow, the child flies on his or her own. Notice the bow, not the arrow, is stretched to a breaking point.

Sometimes we dads get our role (and our kids' role) mixed up; we picture parenting like bows and baskets. Kids are the bows—cute little decorative, dress-up items. We bring them up so pretty, then we place them where we think they can show their best. (What dad doesn't want his child to shine?) After all, when our kids look good, we look good.

Hidden in this misunderstanding of a child, parents become baskets rather than archery bows. We take our children from danger and bring them to us, the basket, the place of safety. We hold, carry, protect, and surround the tender child from life's raging rivers, blistering deserts, and corrupt powers. This can be equated with the connect period of the growing child's life when the child is very dependent upon the parent.

Parents who stay as baskets and keep their children connected as bows eventually become basket cases! The parent is self-absorbed and unable to see the good of letting the child go. Dads (and moms) with weak marriages are especially vulnerable to keeping a child from growing up because the child offers the love and attention the parent is not receiving from his or her spouse. Kids are simply trying to do what they are designed to do: grow up. Dad, be a bow, not a basket.

One of the most difficult results of letting go is watching a child's direction change course midflight and detour from our original target. A lot of kids have told me the last place they want to hit is Dad's target. One sixteen-year-old was point-blank in her words. Interestingly enough, her name is Brianne. I'll let her speak for herself:

Dad, if I choose not to be like you I have the right to do so.

Dad, are you ready to release your child? You've spent years carefully nurturing and shaping the arrow. You've aimed with all your might toward a worthy target. Now, do you trust in the relationship you have invested (or will invest) in your child's first sixteen years of life to guide your child to the target? From what I hear over and over again, our kids want to know. In much simpler words, I have found every teenager (and a fair number of young adults) telling his or her dad, *Trust me. You're ready. Your aim is on target. Dad, it's time to fire.*

Fire: Entrusting Life to Your Child

I've mentioned how A-barriers of anger and absence block us from connecting and relating with our children. Now a final A-barrier stands in the way of this goal: the barrier of authority. One young woman named Lynne is asking her dad to fire away. She said to me,

Although he cares about me, he should give me room to grow into a better person. Dad, you can't hold me back to experience life.

She can't stay "Daddy's little girl" forever. Don't hold back, Dad. You have to fire.

Young people are asking us dads for the keys to their own lives. Are we willing to trust them with those keys? We've been prepared for this day for a long time. Look back with me and consider what transpired:

- Age five: Dad, I asked you to trust me, and you gave me the key to my own skates. I skated, fell, cried, and with your help, I stood up and skated again.
- Age ten: Dad, I asked you to trust me, and you gave me my own key to the house. I opened the door, played loud music, and spilled food in the living room, but you took me in, listened, and lifted me up again.
- Age thirteen: Dad, I asked you to trust me, and you gave me the key to my own locker. I packed my schoolbooks, PE clothes, old food, and too much else in a small space. You helped me study, bought me the right shoes, kept feeding me, and lifted me up again.
- Age sixteen: Dad, I asked you to trust me, and you gave me my key to the car. I drove too fast with all my friends crammed in a car that I could not afford. You supplied

some money to license my new freedom, forgave me when I dented the bumper, and you lifted me up again.

- Age eighteen: Dad, I'm asking you to trust me, and you have given me the key to my life. I am on my own now, but I'm not alone. I know you'll still be around . . .

What happens when we don't trust? We entangle. The opposite of trust is worry. The presence of trust is directly proportionate to the absence of worry, and vice versa. If you want to hear about worry, ask young people about their dads. Here's what I've heard:

Cathy, age fourteen: *I love you, Dad, but don't spend your life worrying about me.*

Heidi, age thirteen: *Dad, lay off and relax. You worry too much.*

Heidi, what color best describes your dad?

Green, my least-favorite color.

I think dad's worry is choking his daughter and making her see the color green. If we listen to these kids, it sounds like we've been given the day off.

Relax. Don't worry. Lay off.

For us to fire our children from the safety of home across the chasm of adolescence to the other side, we must entrust life into our children's hands. Once we see the value of trust, it is time to put power behind the launch.

EMPOWERING YOUR CHILD TO LIFE

I sat with a young teenage girl chatting about her life. I could tell she was dragging a weight in her soul. It was drawing closer to the surface the more we talked. I finally asked her about her relationship with her dad, and like so many times in my conversations with young people, I hit the bull's-eye.

This bright, talented, attractive sixteen-year-old went on to tell me how much she struggled with her dad's inability to trust her. Was she trustworthy? She was a model child—a caring sister, an excellent student, a track star. As a junior, she had a 4.0 grade point average, including many college-level courses. Let me put it this way: You would pay her to influence your kids. But I could tell she was too good. It meant too much for her to know all the right things, say them, and do them.

What came out of her heart was a wish for her dad:

Dad, let me make my own decisions. I'm a good kid with good grades, good habits, good friends, a good boyfriend. . . . Let me go. Just because I want to be with my friends and not with you and Mom doesn't mean I don't love you. Quit smothering me.

How could a dad be so myopic in the raising of his child? It would be easy to jump in and harangue the guy, but a quick revisit to a few of the six adversaries of fatherhood described in Chapter 6 would remind us of the world the young girl faces and make us more understanding of her father's fear. Plus, raising a girl is extremely different from raising a boy. Fathers are frightened to let their young ladies face what is alive and on the prowl. I speak from experience. Soon my daughters will be socializing with fifteen-year-old boys. That ought to be illegal!

Dad, if you are stuck here or get stuck someday soon, it is time to get your *A* of authority out of the way.

The word *fire* has an interesting application: to be released from a job. Dad, part of the ready-aim-fire trio has a message for us dads: *Dad, you're fired.*

May I shoot straight with you? You're losing your job. You are no longer needed on the assembly line. Now is the time to shift positions, pick up the gold watch, and walk proud.

Your paradigm of leadership needs to transfer mantles, from yours to your child's. Be careful and timely in the move, but make the move. As psychologist and radio talk show host Dr. James Dobson wrote, "We must not transfer power too early, even if our children take us daily to the battlefield. On the other hand, we must not retain parental power too long, either."[5]

How do we empower our teenagers to life? Dad, as a founding father with a growing citizenry on your hands, I highly suggest you establish a family constitution to ensure, not only peace, but to bring about the highest possible form of living. If you wait any longer, you'll have a rebellion on your hands, and before you can say, "Boston," your goods will be in the harbor.

To establish a healthy shift of power, a working system needs clarity and understanding of two elements: rights and responsibility. The two-edged sword of rights and responsibility will also provide a balanced safeguard against mutinous, unchecked power.

Clarity of Rights

What rights does your child have as a member of your family? When I speak to parents, I show them a copy of the

United States Constitution and its ten articles of declaration, better known as the Bill of Rights. I ask them, "What rights does a member of your family have regardless of age, ability, power, office?"

Would you be willing to answer the same question for your family? If so, I recommend that you do not do this alone and pass it down like an edict. Gather your family together and ask them the same question: "What rights do we want to give to each other as a member of this family? If your children are too young, create a family bill of rights now and pull it out again when your child hits the preteen years. The experience is a great way to open the curtain of Act 2: Relate.

If your family has no constitution, no purpose statement, no definition of the rights and privileges of its members, is it any surprise to find members on the verge of anarchy or rebellion?

Dad, lead your family to write its own statement as a preamble to your family's bill of rights. Make a mission statement by finishing this sentence:

"Our family exists to . . ."

Then add the ten rights by finishing this statement: "We will accomplish the above mission by empowering each individual with the following ten privileges.

"1. The freedom to . . .

"2. The freedom to . . ." etc.

Freedoms can include the freedom to feel, the freedom to disagree, the freedom to be involved in making rules like curfews. The process alone of writing ten freedoms with your family will infuse a dynamic synergy in all of you. Your kids will feel valued, and they will become family supreme court justices when any right is violated. You may want to hold court if someone feels the loss of a privilege. If you do, don't always be the judge. Let one of the kids don the wig occasionally. Remember, we're trying to *fire* them! Let go, and get out of the way. Work yourself out of a job.

Clarity of Responsibility

I once heard an immigrant say, "What a country this U.S. is. When I heard about the Bill of Rights, I immediately thought there must be a bill of responsibilities." With the exception of paying taxes, the unwritten bill of responsibilities is diminishing in our changing and rapidly declining national culture.

Gather your family in the same fashion you did to establish your family bill of rights, but this time I suggest you embark on a second journey—to write your family bill of responsibilities. Answer this statement: "To be a privileged member of this family with stated rights and to help the family reach the agreed-upon mission, each family member is hereby responsible for the following ten items." You might list things like:

- The responsibility to be honest
- The responsibility to respect other members of the family
- The responsibility to avoid all public insult of any family member and deliver a critique in a spirit of love to better all involved
- The responsibility to listen before I speak

Be as practical or as timely as need be. It would be worth reviewing the family lists of rights and responsibilities each year. Make some fun out of it. Do it around a family retreat or connect it with two nights out on the town.

Before you know it, Dad, the power shift is happening and you've responded to your child's message, *Trust me*. You have entrusted love, hope, and belief in your child and at the same time clearly defined ways for him or her to grow and build his or her character with trustworthiness and responsibility.

A Forewarning

Before I close this chapter, let me show you what lies ahead if you miss the *Trust me* message. A sixteen-year-old girl, Leanne, told me:

My relationship with my dad is a three. Dad, please support my goals. Be proud of me and don't change me.

Leanne let me know that she was teetering on the edge of the *Trust me* message. Sooner than her dad might think, she'll sprint into the next message. For the kids who don't get rights of empowerment, rebellion breaks out. The child who hears no response to the *Trust me* message will communicate more clearly and more loudly, *Let me go.*

I've heard many young people say this to their dads either verbally or nonverbally. They are saying, *Get out of my life.* Some dads are deathly close to being too late. If this is your situation, don't wait too long. You've got just one last message before the line goes dead. If you miss the value of this chapter, you'll experience the cost of the next. Don't be afraid to take the leap of faith.

THE LEAP OF FAITH

My two daughters and I decided to try "The Screamer" at a wonderful camp in California called Hume Lake Camp. The outdoor rappelling course features what I consider nothing less than a one-person roller-coaster ride. The expert staff members strap you into a diaper full of ropes, cables, and clips, and then cinch it tight enough to make your eyes water and your ears ring.

I would go first. The girls would follow.

I was convinced my third child was the end of the line for us, the family caboose, after the young man who was strapping me into the harness made sure I was "safe and secure." (Secure was an understatement!) We were required to wear a helmet also. I know, I know, it is the safe thing to do. But if there really were a chance I could hit a large object with my head to a point of injury, why was I up here? If you're doing it in spite of the brain bucket you just strapped on, you probably have few brain cells worth protecting.

I remember standing on the deck of The Screamer (I was to quickly learn that the activity got its name from the instinctive response victims make due to both the velocity of the plummet to pending death as well as the grab you feel from the rope diaper you're yanked by). The man up top yelled down to the guy below, "Onnn bellllaaayyyy." Then the guy below responded the same, this time only backward. I was searching through my three years of French in school to find out what the heck they had said to each other. I envisioned it to mean something exotic like, "We got another sucker!"

Before I had time to locate my mental French version of

the Webster's dictionary, the guy next to me looked up and said, "Have fun." With that euphemism in mind, I jumped.

I remember the rush of leaving the platform perched a good ten feet above a huge rock, which itself was high enough to make my knees knock. Let me put it this way: The French guy down below, the one in whom I had placed my life, looked more like Pépé le Pew than a human. He was tiny. I remember falling and falling and falling. Ground usually comes quickly as physics go, thirty-two feet per second, if I am not mistaken. The same law was true in this experiment. I recall thinking, "I seem to be drawing closer to the ground than I had first anticipated."

Finally, *finally,* the little French guy, who thought he was bringing me *joie de vivre,* pulled the safety line. My heart would have been relieved had it not been for the cool sensation I immediately experienced in my legs due to the cessation of circulation anywhere below my navel. The "safe and secure" contraption was working just fine, thank you.

I had done The Screamer!

Then I stood watching my six-year-old and my five-year-old daughters. I must admit, they sure looked cute in those helmets. Mind you, no smart father in his right frame of thinking, regardless of fabulous insurance coverage, would believe . . . allow . . . empower . . . trust . . . his children to do such a thing, especially daughters. For some crazy reason, however, I put my trust in the experts' knowledge and my daughters' courage to try. And boy—girl!—did they leap.

What do we adults do? We entrust—hook 'em up with the necessary equipment—and then, we empower—we push 'em off. It is a scary thing to watch your child leap from such heights. But my girls made it, and they loved it. They experienced a feat they never had done before and found a level of courage they did not know they possessed. All it took was a hook and a push, and off they went. I experienced what one young person told me to pass on to his dad:

Dad, I love you and one day I will make you very proud of me when I grow up.

Dear Dad,

I want to grow up. I need your trust to let me try. Please let go. I won't leave you. I'll just become more of me.

Love,
Your child

CHAPTER 11

> *Dear Dad,*
>
> *Leave me alone.*
>
> *Your child*

LEAVE ME ALONE.

I hate the way he treats me and doesn't give me freedom.
Candace, age fourteen

Go away.
Sandrea, age fourteen

I'm going to leave and never come back.
Geoff, age sixteen

Recently my wife and I were perusing carpet samples at one of those home improvement stores. We looked at this one and that one. We sampled the texture of one over the other. I walked with shoes on and shoes off. I did not know so much was involved in saying, "I do" to a mortgage relationship.

Then the salesperson asked what I did for a living. As I usually tell people, I said, "I help teenagers survive adolescence and help parents survive having teenagers in the house." It usually triggers a strong response. This time was no different.

Our salesperson, an attractive woman, initially spoke lightly about her new marriage to her husband, who has a son living with them along with her own daughter. It sounded so nice and congenial, a well-decorated home filled with happiness. The more she talked, however, the more I heard her heart speak.

Soon I sensed struggles in her home the way you might detect a cheap pad beneath new carpet. Our salesperson told me how much her new husband liked to guide his twelve-year-old son to do what was best for him. As she continued, she found listening and empathic ears, so she expressed her concerns over her new stepson's inability to make decisions on his own. She shared how the boy had a tough time functioning at school or other public places because either his dad was not there to tell him what to do or the son feared triggering his dad's wrath. The boy was tacked down in his tracks.

How was the young person responding? As far as I could tell from the stepmom's description, no symptoms of rebellion, detachment, or crisis were apparent. He did what he was supposed to do. Of course he was only twelve. He was just beginning to experiment with the *Trust me* message.

I offered my encouragement to the salesperson/ wife/stepmom. I handed her my card after she inquired about my experience in counseling "families like ours." I said, "If you and your husband would like to meet with me, I'd be available." I briefly talked about my concept of parenting on purpose by establishing a family bill of rights and responsibilities to help raise a responsible, capable, independent person. She was intrigued.

This woman has yet to call me. Will she? Probably not—unless life gets worse. The hurt of her stepson's behavior must stamp out the pain of admitting her (their) parenting weaknesses. When will this occur? When the boy reaches his teen years and begins to communicate his *Trust me* message over and over again. If it goes unheard, he'll reach for a bigger hammer and pound away, *Let me go,* the flip side of *Trust me.* His stepmom will be floored, and this time she won't get compensated for it. She'll pay dearly.

Listen to this letter from Tanya, who is fourteen:

Dear Dad,

I've got my life, my friends, which are not yours and I really need privacy. Something I want to keep to myself. I don't butt into your business, and you stay away from mine. I also hate how you think you know so much about everything I do and how you think you're better friends with my friends than I am.

This chapter isn't long; nor is there a great deal to say. It is not what is said that is important. What strikes hard is the level of intensity behind the kids' message, *Leave me alone!* Maybe you have already heard this message from your child. In your case, you don't need shock treatment; you're well aware of the power behind the voltage. If you haven't heard the cry, imagine if you were a dad to one of the young people below:

You jerk! (Chase, age eleven)
Leave and never speak to me again. (Darrell, age fourteen)
Shape up or ship out. (Andy, age fourteen)
Get away from me. I hate you. (Jesus, age fifteen)
Dad, mind your own business. (Sheri, age twelve)

If we stop and think about it, *Leave me alone* is an absurd message to come from a child who has said over and over again messages like, *I love you, Be with me, Listen to me, Forgive me,* and *Be real with me.* Is this the same child? What has driven him or her to go through nine messages that seem to lean toward Dad, only to catapult to the tenth message, *Leave me alone?*

I find a common response from these young people:

I want away from Dad because there is too much of him in my life. I have an excess of Dad's anger, Dad's absence, and/or Dad's authority. (There are those three *A*s again.)

The A of authority is the final block to a growing child's cry of the heart, *Release me.* Young people, especially those between sixteen and nineteen, are asking you and me to delegate authority to them. Our efforts will not only empower them, but will also head off the pending *Leave me alone* statement. How do we do it?

THE FINAL DEMISE OF THE A OF AUTHORITY

The best way to remove the A of authority is to adopt the *C*s of parenting on purpose: choice, contingency, coach, and consultant.

Choice

My kids get tired of hearing this word. "I know, I know, it's my choice," they say. The more they choose, the more we dads empower them to learn the art of decision making and the prizes or prices that accompany these decisions. The effectiveness of raising a responsible child will rise or fall on this one word. I could list application after application of how dads can maximize the power of their child's choices, but the common thread is this: Children become responsible as they have the power to make age-appropriate decisions and experience directly the consequences, good or bad, of those choices.[1]

If the word *choice* hasn't been a part of your vocabulary before, employ it now.

Contingency

Today's marketplace is being transformed by the contingency employee. More employers than ever before are hiring part-time or seasonal workers. Dad, you and I are contingency workers. True, once a dad, forever a dad. (The good and bad news is you can't divorce your dad. Even if a dad is absent, his presence is strong.) The role of an effective father, however, changes continually. His part is contingent upon the needs, age, messages, and cries of the child's heart.[2] Dad, look at yourself as a Dad Friday, a temp father. Again, you do not abandon the position as dad, you just change your roles. That's where the next two words come into play.

Coach

The role of the coach is to encourage and to guide a player to win. The coach is never the player unless you are referring to a player/coach, a thing of the past. Even then, the position was on a team; there were still other individual players.

Dad, you move to coach when your child moves to the teenage years. Shift your energies from teaching the basics to a rookie to coaching both basic and advanced techniques. There may have been a time you were the model player, but understand the change. Now you are a coach, and coaches don't play. Some dads can be as effective by sitting

in the bleachers and letting go. Actor/director Kevin Cost-
ner had this to say about his dad:

> I think I like sports because of my father. He never insisted I
> play, which made it even more attractive. He's my ideal of
> how a father should direct his son. Sports, besides the obvi-
> ous competitive aspect, is about sharing and being fair. And
> I've always liked to roll in the dirt.[3]

Consultant

Ever notice how guys who used to be coaches now
consult? There's wisdom in the change. (Or they become
color commentators on TV. I'm yet to find that job for
retired dads.) A consultant is an expert in a field who is hired
to provide specific guidance for a certain area of need. Two
elements apply to consulting: First, consultants are respected
for their expertise. They know what they are talking about,
and good consultants keep their advice limited to their
experience. Second, every consultant is brought in. Consultants never force their way in; dictators and vigilantes do.

If your child is not asking for advice, he or she will
probably not be listening to your guidance. When your child
is ten, you are the captain, so you play your part to communicate your point. When your child is eighteen, wait until
his or her need (pain) prompts him or her to spend some
valuable resources bringing in the consultant.

Recall the words *ready, aim, fire!* The word *fire* was the
empowering given to a child by his or her dad. Remember,
fire also means to let go or get fired from a job. Dad, if we
don't resign, we are going to get fired.

What will our salesperson's twelve-year-old stepson do if his father doesn't hear his *Trust me* message?

I'll let Angie and Geoff, ages thirteen and sixteen, respond:

Angie: *I'm going to run away.*

Geoff: *I'm going to leave and never come back.*

I've learned not to take their words lightly. These are not idle threats. With thousands of youths running away each year, the streets are filled with Angies and Geoffs who never convinced Dad how serious they really were. If they don't leave before they graduate from high school, they end up leaving under the guise of college or career—and taking their hearts far away from home, even if they only move across town or to the other end of the state. They are gone.

Building a bridge across a chasm is no longer a simple task. Sixteen-plus years of anger, absence, and/or authority between the dad and the child will make a major strategy necessary to bring the two back together. It is time for a helicopter to cover significant ground if Dad wants a relationship with this child. The work will demand the guidance of professionals. Like a squad of Navy Seals or Green Berets, Dad needs special tactics and weapons to bring home the family MIA.

What does the father of an MIA do? Are you a dad who has realized your child is saying the message that makes up the center of this chapter, *Leave me alone?* Will you admit you have controlled your child too long and too strong and now your child no longer wants you around? Until a country realizes it has a soldier missing in action, it will never mount an effort to bring the soldier home.

Dad, remember, you are a founding father of a country

in your name. The citizens will act according to the national constitution. If you've neglected to offer human rights to someone in your family, he or she feels violated. You can't just walk in and say, "Come back home. All is well." It will take a strategic effort on your part to bring the heart of your child home. And it will demand your energy, effort, and self-sacrifice. Is the end result of a true relationship with your child worth the effort? It's your time to choose, Dad.

And don't stop here. This is by far the most difficult chapter in the entire book. Hear me: There is hope! Countless father-child relationships come back from the chasm of despair to a reconciled status. If you feel the symptoms of *Leave me alone* in your home, I recommend that you reread the last chapter, which serves to build the vital release phase of your young person's development.

THE POWER OF THE POSITION

President Ronald Reagan faced a trying time in our nation's history as he heralded the Cold War into its final chapter. The Soviet Union was considered by many to be our greatest enemy over the past sixty-five years except for a brief alliance during World War II. In his dealing with the Russians, Reagan represented a society that believed in human rights, freedom, and democracy. At the height of the dilemma, Reagan called the USSR the "evil empire."

Global-ranged nuclear weapons stared down the barrel at every American, whether he or she was sitting at a negotiating table in Geneva or at a kitchen table in Kansas. If an attack was imminent, the United States had the firepower to act. If the decision was to be made, the president was the man to decide.

Reagan wrote, "As President, I carried no wallet, no money, no driver's license, no keys. But wherever I went, I carried a small plastic-coated card, and a military aide was always close by carrying a small bag referred to as 'the football.' It contained directives for launching our nuclear weapons, and the plastic card listed codes confirming that it was actually the President of the U.S. who was ordering the unleashing of these weapons. The decision to launch was mine alone to make."[4]

In the hand of one man lies the national security for the United States. The decision is his alone to make. Dad, you've heard it from the beginning; hear it again now. You matter to your child. You have tremendous influence over the young life placed in your hands. Your authority will greatly influence the future well-being of your child. If you hold on too long and too strong, you will force the child out of your life. If Reagan had let his authority override his reasoning and best interest for the country, 150,000,000 Americans would have died. And that is if we had won.[5]

You hold a tremendous amount of power in the palm of your hand, Dad. Caution is warranted to not misappropriate your position. Don't wait until you hear these words from one young man who remained anonymous:

Dad, you are nothing to this family, and you are losing your son and are not part of my life anymore.

Sadly enough, his dad is now an anonymous figure in the young man's life.

Another comment from a sixteen-year-old girl also caught my attention. She wanted her dad to know,

Trust me to do what's right because I can do things right.

Her name is Jami. I'm all ears with this girl. You see, I've got a six-year-old girl in my life whose name is Jamie. I have only ten years to connect, relate, and then begin to release my Jamie. One day I will have a young person saying, "Dad, trust me to do what is right." If I don't listen, she'll say, "Leave me alone." If I let it go that far, she may never return. That's a cold war I want to avoid at all costs.

Dear Dad,

I need you beside me, not in front of me. If you don't move, soon you'll be in back of me. I need encouragement not control. Please let me go so we can stay together, otherwise I'm on my own . . . and so are you.

Love,
Your child

PART

FIVE

THE KIDS' EPIPHANY:

Thanks, Dad. I love you!

WHAT KIDS SAY . . .

I really appreciate everything you've done for me, and I love you very much.

Mandy, age sixteen

I appreciate him for always loving me like a daughter and always putting up with me.

Natasha, age thirteen

I would never trade you for any other dad in the world because you're the best.

Randy, age fourteen

WHAT KIDS MEAN . . .

Thanks, Dad.

I love you.

WHAT KIDS NEED . . .

A dad who is willing to accept his children's gratitude.

CHAPTER 12

Dear Dad,

　Thank you for being you.

Love,
Your child

THANKS, DAD. I LOVE YOU!

Thanks for being a great dad.
Mike, age twelve

Thank you for everything you ever did.
Michelle, age seventeen

God bless you. I love you.
Jason, age fifteen

Jon pulled out the piece of paper as if it were a medal from a sports trophy case. I could tell by the way he presented it to my friend Rik and I that Jon was filled with pride. I would have thought he was about to share a Pulitzer Prize–winning masterpiece.

"Listen to what my daughter submitted in her class in response to an essay project," Jon said. And then he read on.

My dad is a developer. In this time, that is not a very good occupation. All the bankers are afraid to give loans because of the economy. My dad has been trying for at least two years to get a loan for one of his projects. He owns his own business, so he doesn't really get a steady paycheck. Through all of this, he is patient, kind, and still keeps his sense of humor. . . .

One of my dad's other great qualities is his creativity and his fun attitude. It doesn't sound important, but believe me it is. His sense of humor makes him fun to be around. I guess you could call him weird also. He rides his rollerblades to and from work (about seven miles each way), or he'll ride his bike (then he'll take the long way). It is unusual when he drives. We have about sixteen bicycles in our garage for the four of us.

My dad designed our house; it is great! It has steel beams running through it, and the outside is made of all cedar. He came home from work one night on his rollerblades, and started swinging on our metal beams. My dad's sense of humor has made him fun to be around and has gotten him through a lot.

My dad's patience, kindness, and sense of humor have gotten him far. He has a lot of other great qualities, but these three are the strongest. For my dad's sake, I hope he never has to use those three traits like he has in these past two years.

Jon, Rik, and I stood in momentary silence. As fathers of eleven kids in our three families, we all understood the value of this literary masterpiece, especially when written by a teenager. I would venture to guess Rik had the same thoughts I did: *One day I hope to receive such a gift from my child.*

When inspired by a class assignment, Kelly discovered the value of her dad. She'd had a flash of insight. Her words defining her dad's valuable character qualities can be summarized in one phrase: *Thanks, Dad!*

THE EPIPHANY

Our journey through kids' hearts has come to its final act. I have named this scene the "Epiphany." Like the credits rolling after a movie, or the recognition of the conductor and orchestra after a concert, or the actors bowing on the stage after a live theater production, the drama closes with applause from the audience.

Epiphany is a celebration in the Christian church that is held on January 6 and commemorates both the revealing of Jesus as the Christ to the Gentiles (when the wise men from afar visit Him) and also the baptism of Jesus. Generally speaking, Webster's dictionary defines epiphany as, "a moment of sudden intuitive understanding; a flash of insight." The epiphany is not only the discovery, but also the response.

The *Dear Dad* epiphany occurs when a child realizes the presence, power, and value of his or her father and then expresses this understanding to Dad. This whole book is really an epiphany—insight about us dads from our kids—even though some of the material has been difficult and challenging.

Dads, we matter. Our kids need and want us. They desire to connect with and relate to us. Once we hear these messages and respond to them as best we can, our children ask for a loving release. Throughout the entire journey, our children are saying, *Thanks, Dad. You matter to me, then and now.*

Child after child has helped me realize how many of them are grateful for their dads. As I jokingly tell them when I speak to young people, "If it weren't for your dad and mom . . . you wouldn't be here." All kidding aside, they know that, and many are grateful because of it.

Dad, it's now time to switch roles. It is your turn to be on stage. If you listen closely and peer through the spotlight that has been on you for the past eleven chapters, you will see your child rise from the seat and applaud. You deserve the credit.

THANKS TO DAD

Few words from all the comments of more than fifteen hundred surveys and fifteen years of youth work say thank you as clearly, succinctly, and strongly as sixteen-year-old Chris:

Thanks for being the dad a lot of other guys want and need.

With Chris's initial accolade, let's listen to the kids' applause:

- Marcy, age sixteen: *I really appreciate everything you've done for me and I love you very much.*
- Jeremy, age eighteen: *Thanks for being there.*
- Megan, age fourteen: *My relationship with my dad is a nine. He's wonderful.*
- Natalie, age thirteen: *I appreciate him for always loving me like a daughter and always putting up with me.*

It seems like Natalie's dad had to work to always be there for his daughter.

Epiphany is a discovery of something that's momentous, insightful, or godlike. Often coupled with this appearance of greatness is the awareness of the self in light of the other. For Natalie, her gratitude for her dad grew when she realized that fathering her takes patience, forgiveness, courage, and a list of other resources. Regardless of who she was and what she did, Natalie's dad never let her be removed from her status as his daughter. She always remained connected. For that she is grateful.

Thirty-four people, approximately 3 percent of the fifteen hundred surveyed, used the word *perfect* to describe their relationship with their fathers. Most of them applied the word to the question, "Rate your relationship with your dad on a scale of one to ten."

One young woman brought greatness to the extreme in saying,

My dad is perfect so he is the color white.

You may be thinking what first came to my mind—probably some young preteenager yet to experience the real dad. The author of the quote is seventeen. I will give her dad the benefit of the doubt since seventeen years is plenty of time to let the cat out of the bag.

Jessica, age sixteen, had the same response. She said,

My relationship with my dad is a ten. It's perfect.

(At least she gives her dad room to not have to be perfect. What they have created together is perfect, not just her dad alone.)

Laurie, age twelve, elevates her dad to the peak of greatness. She says,

My dad is the color white because I think of heaven. If I could tell him anything, I would say, "Thank you, Dad, and I love you."

Do kids expect dads to walk on water? Not from what I've heard them tell me. Like Alexandra, age thirteen, many of them said simply,

Thank you for being the best dad you can be.

Kent, age thirteen, applies the color white to his dad, but

he doesn't hear angels sing when he thinks of Dad. For Kent, white means,

My dad is as white as snow and snow is cool.

Fourteen-year-old Ryan would never give up his dad:

I would never trade you for any other dad in the world because you're the best.

Another superdad you presume? Just ask Ryan.

My dad is a regular dad who cares for me very much.

What's his dad's secret? No super-unleaded dad, just extra care when it is time for a fill-up. It's customer service, not superb product, that keeps Ryan's dad out of the commodity trading pit. Jeremy, age seventeen, says the same about the business of dad-trading,

I wouldn't trade my dad for anyone.

One anonymous comment stated,

I appreciate his love and dedication to my mother and I.

I hope this is one kid who does not keep his or her comments anonymous from his or her dad. I would hate to see such a powerful statement go unheard.

A GATHERING FOR THE EPIPHANY

Dad, the list goes on and on. I could fill a sanctuary with more than one hundred people who want to offer up their words of thanks at this epiphany celebration. From a girl named Amber to a boy named Zach, from eleven-year-old Matt to forty-year-old Cynthia, there are too many to list one by one. The audience is filled with hundreds of hands applauding with a message from the heart. The total crowd together creates a thundering choir of gratitude and shouts of *Bravo!*

More important than the masses are the one or two kids in the front row. When I am at the end of my life and the final curtain closes, Brookelyn, Jamie, and Chase will be the most important critics in the audience. If I can hear them utter, *Thanks!* my time on earth will have been well invested.

Dear Dad,

   You matter. Thank you for being my dad.

Love,
Your child

R E S O U R C E S

F O R   A   H U R T I N G   D A D

Books

Arterburn, Stephen. *Addicted to "Love."* Ann Arbor, MI: Servant,1991.

Arterburn, Stephen, and Jim Burns. *Drug-Proof Your Kids . . . And Help Them Say No.* Colorado Springs, CO: Focus on the Family, 1989.

Cloud, Henry, and John Townsend. *Boundaries: Gaining Control of Your Life.* Grand Rapids: Zondervan, 1992.

The Holy Bible, the New King James Version. Nashville: Thomas Nelson, 1990.

The Life Recovery Bible. Wheaton, IL: Tyndale, 1992.

Minirth, Dr. Frank, Dr. Paul Meier, Dr. Robert Hemfelt, and Dr. Sharon Sneed. *Love Hunger.* Nashville: Thomas Nelson, 1990.

Smedes, Lewis B. *Forgive and Forget: Healing the Hurts We Don't Deserve.* San Francisco: Harper, 1991.

Stoop, David, and James Masteller. *Forgiving Our Parents, Forgiving Ourselves.* Ann Arbor, MI: Servant, 1991.

Stoop, David, and Steve Arterburn. *The Angry Man.* Dallas: Word, 1991.

Warren, Neil Clark. *Making Anger Your Ally.* Colorado Springs: Focus on the Family, 1993.

Organizations

Alcoholics Anonymous or other twelve-step groups:
Consult your phone book for local listings.

Fathernet: On-line computer access
(612) 626-1212, cyfec@staff.tc.umn.edu.

Focus on the Family
420 N. Cascade Avenue
Colorado Springs, CO 80903
(719) 531-3400

Minirth Meier New Life Treatment Centers
1-800-NEW-LIFE

The National Center for Fathering
Ken Canfield, Founder
10200 W. 75th, Suite 267
Shawnee Mission, KS 66204
(913) 384-4661 or (800) 593-DADS

The National Institute of Youth Ministry
P.O. Box 4374
San Clemente, California 92674
(714) 498-4418

Promise Keepers (national men's organization)
P.O. Box 18376
Boulder, CO 80308
(303) 421-2800

Your local church

N O T E S

Chapter 1

1. Richard Nixon, *In the Arena,* ed. Julie Rubenstein (New York: Pocket Books, 1991), 10.

Chapter 2

1. "The Living Years," written by Mike Rutherford and B. A. Robertson, copyright Atlantic Recording Corp., administered by Hidden Pun Music, Inc.

Chapter 3

1. Richard Lacayo, "Violence Is Up," *Time,* 7 February 1994, 52–53.
2. Social worker Melissa Manning, quoted in Nancy R. Gibbs, "Bringing Up Father," *Time,* 18 June 1993, 55.
3. Susan E. Kuhn, "Teenagers Talk About Life," *Fortune,* 10 August 1992, 55.
4. Stephen R. Covey, *Seven Habits of Highly Effective People* (New York: Fireside, 1990), 188–99.
5. Ibid.
6. Al Reis and Jack Trout, *The 22 Immutable Laws of Marketing* (New York: Harper Business, 1993).
7. 1 Timothy 3:5.
8. David Gelman, "A Much Riskier Passage," *Newsweek Special Issue, The New Teens: What Makes Them Different?* June 1990, 8–10.
9. Ibid.
10. Ibid.
11. Ibid.
12. Christopher Hall, "Holy Health," *Christianity Today,* 23 November 1992, 21.
13. Ibid.

14. Vern E. Smith with David Gelman, "Two Dads and a Dream—But No Illusions," *Newsweek*, 30 August 1993, 21.
15. Drawn Chris Foster, "Syracuse's McCorkle Finds a Comfort Zone," *Los Angeles Times,* 18 February 1994.

Chapter 4
1. Center for Disease Prevention and Control (Atlanta), "Suicide Fact Sheet," 11 March 1994, 1.
2. Covey, *Seven Habits,* 1-340.
3. Proverbs 13:24.
4. Proverbs 14:17.
5. Proverbs 29:22.
6. Proverbs 29:11.
7. Proverbs 13.20.
8. Proverbs 1:7.

Chapter 5
1. Norman Cousins, *Head First: The Biology of Hope* (New York: Dutton Signet, 1990), and *Anatomy of an Illness* (New York: Bantam, 1983).
2. Matthew 19:14.
3. The Bible offers many powerful pictures of a life-saver. One of my favorites is Matthew 14:22–33.

Chapter 6
1. Tim Hansel, *What Kids Need Most in a Dad* (Grand Rapids: Revell, 1989), 11.
2. Peter Newcomb, "Hey Dude, Let's Consume," *Forbes,* 11 June 1990, 126ff.
3. Mark Hunter, "Where's Papa?" *Men's Health,* July/August 1993, 26–27.
4. Myron Magnet, "The American Family," *Fortune,* 10 August 1992, 123.
5. Ibid.
6. For a comprehensive study on this topic see David Stoop, *Making Peace with Your Father* (Wheaton, IL: Tyndale House, 1992).
7. Yankelovich Clancy Shulman survey of eighteen- to twenty-four-

year-olds, reported in Ann Blackman, Elizabeth Taylor, and James Wilwerth, "The Road to Equality," *Time,* Fall 90, 14.

8. For more ideas on managing family finances, refer to Larry Burkett, *Business by the Book* (Nashville: Thomas Nelson, 1990), Burkett's *Master Your Money* (Nashville: Thomas Nelson, 1991), and Ron Blue, *Storm Shelter* (Nashville: Thomas Nelson, 1994).

9. Blackman, et al., "The Road to Equality," 14.

10. Thomas Peters and Nancy Austin, *A Passion for Excellence* (New York: Warner Books, 1985), 495–96.

11. Quoted in Covey, *Seven Habits,* 201.

12. Wally Joyner, Kansas City Royals first baseman as quoted in Linda Konner, "What My Father Taught Me," *Men's Health,* June 1992, 75.

13. Contact Paul Lewis at Family University, P.O. Box 270616, San Diego, California 92198-1616.

14. Dan Russell, quoted in Elizabeth Mehren's "On the Daddy Track," *Los Angeles Times,* 30 June 1993.

15. Virginia Bellafonte, "Lineman with Snugli," *Time,* 1 November 1993, 101.

16. Dr. Charlie Shedd, *A Dad Is for Spending Time With* (Kansas City, MO: Sheed, Andrews, and McMeel, Inc., 1978), 12.

17. *President's Circle Fax Letter* (Tustin, CA), 20 June 1994, 1.

Chapter 7

1. Louis S. Richman, "Struggling to Save Our Kids," *Fortune,* 10 August 1992, 136.

Chapter 8

1. Chuck Swindoll, *Seasons of Life* (Portland, OR: Multnomah Press, 1983), 71.

2. Cousins, *Head First: The Biology of Hope,* 111.

3. Ibid.

4. M. Scott Peck, *People of the Lie* (New York: Simon & Schuster, 1983), 150.

5. "The Last Song," written by Elton John and Bernie Taupin, copyright Big Pig Music Ltd., administered by Interson USA, Inc.

6. Craig MacFarlane, interview by Robert Schuller, *Hour of Power*, Crystal Cathedral Ministries, no date available.

7. See the Bible, 1 John 1:9 and Romans 5:8.

8. Robert K. Greenleaf, *Servant Leadership* (New York: Paulist Press, 1977), 21.

Chapter 9

1. Quoted in Chuck Swindoll, *Dropping Your Guard* (New York: Bantam, 1987), 117.

2. From *Heartland Samples for Father* (Edina, CA: Heartland Samples Inc., 1991).

3. In my seminar on today's youth culture, I suggest:

Young people are suffering from . . .	Young people are looking for . . .
Superficiality	Authenticity
Anonymity	Intimacy
Complexity	Simplicity
Monotony	Significance
Secularity	Spirituality

4. Mark Robichaux, "Next They'll Tell Us Gene Kelly Wasn't Really Singing in the Rain," *Wall Street Journal*, 24 May 1990.

5. Ibid.

6. Ibid.

7. Ibid.

8. Ibid.

9. Bill Plaschke, "The Good Son," *Los Angeles Times*, 7 December 1993.

10. Konner, "What My Father Taught Me," 75.

11. Harvey MacKay, *Beware of the Naked Man Who Offers You His Shirt* (New York: Morrow, 1990), 384.

12. C. S. Lewis, *Surprised by Joy* (New York: Harcourt Brace Jovanovich, 1955), 184.

13. ———, *The Lion, The Witch, and The Wardrobe* (London: Harper-Collins, 1950), 146–47.

Chapter 10

1. Konner, "What My Father Taught Me," 73.
2. For more information on Prison Fellowship or the writing and speaking of Chuck Colson, contact Prison Fellowship, P.O. Box 17500, Washington, D.C. 20041-0500.
3. Chuck Colson, *Against the Night* (Ann Arbor: Servant, 1991), 77.
4. I tip my hat to M. Scott Peck and his book *A World Waiting to Be Born* (New York: Bantam, 1993), 147–72, for the imagery of parenting as bows and arrows. Of course, many of us have drawn the concept from the Bible: "Like arrows in the hand of a warrior, / So are the children of one's youth. / Happy is the man who has his quiver full of them" (Ps. 127:4–5). Also refer to Stu Weber's *Tender Warrior* (Sisters, OR: Questar, 1993) for further application of the image of children like arrows in the hand of a warrior/dad.
5. James Dobson, *Parenting Isn't for Cowards* (Waco, TX.: Word, 1987), 125.

Chapter 11

1. Foster Cline and Jim Fay, *Parenting with Love and Logic* (Colorado Springs, CO: NavPress, 1990). This is one of the finest books I have read on raising responsible children.
2. For an insightful presentation of the changing roles a dad takes through the years, refer to Dr. David Stoop, *Making Peace with Your Father* (Wheaton, IL: Tyndale, 1992).
3. Konner, "What My Father Taught Me," 73.
4. Ronald Reagan, *An American Life* (New York: Simon and Schuster, 1990), excerpted in *Time*, 5 November 1990, 62.
5. Ibid.